Author and Creative Director: Andrea Hungerford
Photographer: Jenn Bakos
Production Editor: Hannah Thiessen
Patterns and Projects Designers: Makenzie Alvarez, Amy Christoffers, Andrea Hungerford, Ellen Mason, Angela Tong, Nataliya Volyanyuk
Pattern Technical Editors: Meaghan Corwin and Alexandra Viegel
Models: Martha Cornwell, Andrea Hungerford, Danica Morris, Hannah Thiessen
Map painted in acrylics by Hannah Thiessen
Printer: B&B Print Source

ORDERING INFORMATION
By Hand is published three times annually. Subscriptions or single-issue purchases can be ordered online at: www.byhandserial.com.

Wholesale inquiries may be submitted via e-mail to www.nnkpress.com (North American distribution) or julie.asselin@yahoo.ca (Canadian distribution).

Published by Blueberry Hill
www.byhandserial.com
info@byhandserial.com

You can also find us on:
Ravelry at www.ravelry.com/groups/by-hand-serial
Facebook at www.facebook.com/byhandserial
Instagram at www.instagram.com/byhandserial

PRINTED IN THE USA
This book is printed on sustainably sourced paper at a wind-power optioned facility that practices 100% recycling of all waste materials. The paper in this publication contains fibers from well managed and responsibly harvested forests that meet strict environmental and socioeconomic standards.

FIRST EDITION
Winter 2020

Cover photo: The village of Harrisville, New Hampshire

By Hand
making communities

Lookbook No. 11: Vermont and New Hampshire

Table Of Contents

Making Communities   3

Harrisville Designs   5

Knitting Pattern:
Harrisville Barn Jacket   12

Wing and a Prayer Farm   21

Baking: Pearway to Heaven   26

Knitting Pattern:
Beyond the Maples   32

Alice Ogden Black Ash Baskets   39

Odacier Knitting and Sewing Patterns   43

Sewing Project:
Sarah Ann Tunic   46

The Woolly Thistle   51

Knitting Pattern:
Spruce Peak Pullover   56

Green Mountain Spinnery   63

Sewing Project:
Falling Leaves   68

Marshfield School of Weaving   73

Knitting Pattern:
Winter Light   78

Dianne Shullenberger   85

Knitting Pattern:
Golden Afternoon Mittens   88

Glossary   92

Author/Creative Director Andrea Hungerford

Andrea Hungerford loves knitting for both the solitude it provides and the community it builds. Most all of her remaining time is spent with her three teenage daughters, who have taught her to navigate and even occasionally embrace the crazy chaos of everyday life. Her summertime homes away from home are the San Juan Islands and the coast of Maine, and her favorite place to scuba dive is Turks & Caicos, where she once swam with a whale shark. She hates to cook but loves to bake, and learns to navigate any new city she visits by locating the best bakery in town and going from there. She has cultivated a large and unwieldy garden at her home in the countryside, and loves to pick lilacs and peonies in the spring, sweet cherry tomatoes in the summer, and pink, red, and orange dahlias in the fall. She cares passionately about the environment and believes that there is no greater cause than protecting the natural world for future generations.

Photographer Jenn Bakos

Jenn Bakos is full time photographer from the seacoast of New Hampshire whose work focuses on food, lifestyle, small business, and weddings. She attended Hallmark Institute of Photography in Western Massachusetts and continued on to internships in San Francisco and back in New Hampshire before starting her own business. Outside of photography you can usually find her camping, kayaking, and bike riding around New England or searching for the best local coffee shops and scenic views.

Production Editor Hannah Thiessen

Southern-born and bred, Hannah Thiessen is a self-proclaimed yarn obsessive, dabbling in knitting, crochet, weaving, spinning and sewing. She works day-to-day in the yarn industry, helping brands realize their creative potential, and is the author of *Slow Knitting*, a book focused on the beauty of making by hand. In her role as *By Hand Serial's* Production Editor, Hannah coordinates our designs and drives the visuals for our styled shoots and social media.

Making Communities

I have trouble with monogamy. That is, I'm never satisfied with being married to just one creative endeavor. As long as I can remember, my passion for making follows a traditional arc: head-over-heels infatuation, followed by the development of some degree of competency (if not mastery), and then I find a new art form and I head off in a totally different direction. Every time I see something new, I want to try it. It's like waving a shiny toy in front of me.

My failure to commit goes against the grain, I'm afraid. We are told that it is increasingly important in this day and age to specialize. Find your passion. Delve deep, develop expertise in your field. Even at a young age, kids are encouraged, even required to specialize. After elementary school (or even earlier), they can't play a different sport each season - they're supposed to pick just one and play it year-round. If they don't specialize, they'll never be competitive, never make it on the best teams, never be taken seriously as an athlete. It's no different in academics - students are supposed to figure out what they're interested in by high school, so they can pick the right college, so they have a clear track to graduate school, so they can get an early jump on a career that will require a great deal of specialization in order to rise to the top of their field. Everywhere I look, the message is to pick a path and stick to it. In fast-paced, achievement-oriented, results-based modern life, there is little encouragement to experiment, explore, or wander *a la* Jack Kerouac.

In the face of all of this subliminal messaging, I worry that my lack of monogamy means that I am unfocused, or that I will never develop proficiency at anything in particular. Will I just dabble with this and that, always moving on before I really get the hang of it? At some point, will I run out of creative endeavors I want to experiment with, or will my well of creativity just dry up?

Over time, though, I've come to conclude that the opposite is true. Learning new skills, experimenting with new passions, is not only creativity in action, but it sparks creativity, as well. I might not be the world's foremost expert in any particular field, and I suppose that might limit opportunities available to me. But it gives me a greater appreciation for makers in a wide variety of fields, and it reminds me how important it is to be a lifelong learner. Learning is one of those skills that, as we get older, gets more and more difficult. We can choose to settle in to our comfort zone - specialization allows us to explore deeply something we are already familiar with - but it doesn't necessarily stretch us in new and unfamiliar directions. And the more we fall out of the practice of learning new things, the more difficult it gets. Because learning is painful. It is failure, missteps, asking embarrassing questions, and working for long hours on something that doesn't turn out as we intended. But it is also embracing imperfection, celebrating process over product, and a willingness to be vulnerable. Learning something new isn't necessarily pretty, but it is one of the best possible ways to keep our minds and our spirits stretching and growing.

So to all of you creative polygamists out there, I say, let's celebrate the next time we head down a new crafting rabbit hole! At least, that's what I tell myself as I stare admiringly at a shiny new Harrisville floor weaving loom and scheme how I will fit in weaving lessons in the upcoming year . . .

Warmly,
Andrea

3

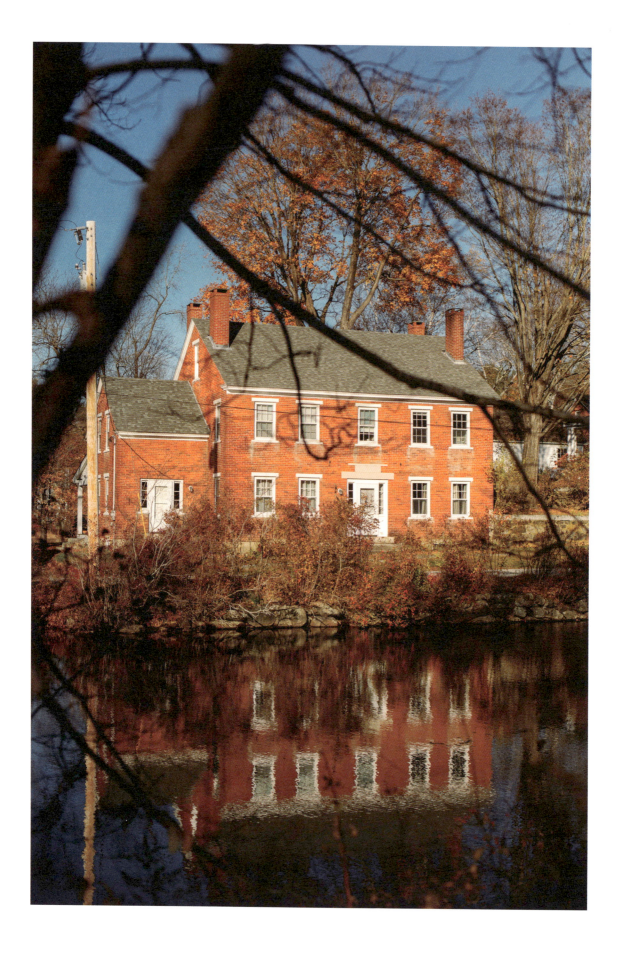

Harrisville Designs

Almost two decades into the 21st century, many small towns in New England are struggling to find balance between the past and the future. How to hold on to what is historically valuable, and blend it with an eye toward what lies ahead? Extracting the best parts of our history and melding tradition with advancements toward a more sustainable and equitable future is not an easy task, and one that many mill towns across the Northeast are struggling to address.

Nowhere has this delicate balancing act been accomplished more successfully than the village of Harrisville, New Hampshire. Harrisville has managed to preserve the stately beauty and close-knit community of its roots, while at the same time, creating a plan for the future and supporting a company that shows great foresight and promise for years to come.

This was not an easy accomplishment, by any means. In fact, the history of Harrisville over more than 200 years has been one of challenging times and difficult decisions. In the last years of the 18th century, drawn by the easy availability of water power, the Harris family established a textile mill, erecting many of the buildings that housed the mill and its workers that still stand today. The woolen industry became the lifeblood of the community, employing much of the village population. In the mid-1800s, the Colony family purchased the holdings and founded Cheshire Mills, which became one of the last New England textile mills in operation by the time it closed in 1970.

This could have been the death knell for the historic village. As Nick Colony, the sixth generation of the Colony Family to run the Harrisville mill recalls, his grandfather fought hard to keep the textile company

open when every other mill in New England was going out of business. "The mill would close periodically, but always reopened when business rebounded. The work bell would ring, and everyone would know that the mill was open again. In 1970, when it closed for good, Harrisville was in danger of becoming either a museum or an industrial park."

Instead, the town took what was a radical approach at that time – a handful of locals and preservationists formed Historic Harrisville, a non-profit organization that purchased the buildings to preserve them, and then leased them out to pay for the costs of upkeep. As a result, Harrisville Village was designated as a National Historic Landmark in 1977, as the only 19th century textile village in America still in its original form.

Only a year after the mill closed, John J. Colony III (known to everyone in Harrisville as Chick) opened Harrisville Designs, to keep the textile tradition alive and to ensure the economic viability of the town and its citizens. Harrisville Designs originally focused on milling wool yarns for hand weavers, using New Zealand merino cross

wools. As knitting began to see a resurgence, Chick began adding in a much softer Australian wool to appeal to hand knitters. Today, Harrisville Designs custom blends all of its own colors by mixing dyed-in-the-wool fleece. In addition to its own yarn lines, Harrisville Designs also mills yarns for other labels, including Brooklyn Tweed, Jill Draper, and Peace Fleece.

On the autumn day that we visited Harrisville, it felt like stepping into a New England postcard. The tiny village is a cluster of red brick and stone buildings, tucked into a small pocket of woodland around Harrisville pond. The Harrisville General Store sits up on a hill, serving as a communal gathering center and supplying the community

6

with its morning coffee, fresh-baked pastries, and a mouth-watering lunch menu. We spent a fascinating morning touring the mill buildings and listening to Chick regale us with stories of the past fifty years of trials and tribulations. The Harrisville Designs operations are spread out among both historic and more recently erected buildings, each seemingly larger than the last. In addition to the extensive process of milling yarn, Harrisville Designs has diversified to include a woodworking shop, where floor looms in various sizes are constructed. The looms are designed so that they can be shipped in surprisingly small boxes, with clear assembly instructions that allow weavers to gain a fundamental understanding of their equipment. The company also produces the Friendly Loom Product line for children (and adults!), elevating the craft of making potholders by focusing on much higher quality materials like metal looms and cotton loops.

Chick carries the entire history of Harrisville Designs in his head, and clearly knows the ins and outs of every facet of the operation. He greets all of the employees with a friendly familiarity, and it's evident that the mill plays a central role in providing good employment for the local residents, which remains as important today as it was historically. Chick's business acumen over the past fifty years has helped the company weather extreme changes in the textile industry by successfully diversifying to serve many different populations of crafters. It has become a one-stop source for all fiber-related crafts: weaving, knitting, crocheting, felting, spinning, rug hooking, needlepoint, and more.

The on-site retail store is a lovely historic room with old wooden floors, high ceilings, and beautiful natural light. Everywhere you look is color, and everything you touch is authentic woolly texture. The sales staff is gracious and knowledgeable; I listen to them chat with a wide variety of customers who stream in through the door, welcoming everyone from tour buses of senior citizens to knitters and weavers who have traveled long distances to touch the yarns and see where they are made. Many of the visitors don't even make with yarn; they

are just fascinated by the story of the mill town, and eager to visit the lovely village.

Six generations of the Colony family have run Harrisville Designs, including two of Chick's three sons. If Chick is the history and operational knowledge of Harrisville Designs, his son Nick is the visionary. Nick has worked various jobs at the mill since he was 16 years old; however, his decision to return to the business after

college and become part of the next generation of the Colony family to run the company wasn't pre-ordained. Both father and son emphasize that none of the Colony children were ever pressured to join the family business. This can't have been easy for the Colony parents, to leave options open for their children after five generations of investment in the town and the textile industry. But Chick and his wife Patricia were determined not to make that decision for any of their children. As a result, Nick recalls, "once I decided that I really wanted to give the company a look, and once they knew I was genuinely excited about it, that it was a decision I came to on my own terms, they welcomed me."

In 2009, Nick moved back into the house where he grew up and began his "formal" Harrisville Designs education. "My dad wanted me to work with every single employee for at least a week or two, to learn the business from the inside out." Both father and son speak highly of each other, lauding what the other brings to the business, and walking that careful balance of pairing experience with new ideas. Nick draws from Chick's experience and institutional knowledge, and Chick values Nick's marketing and business background and the cutting-edge ideas and concepts that he brings to an industry that is often too mired in tradition to change with the times.

In the past decade, Nick's on-the-job education has allowed him to appreciate not only the company's history and its current achievements, but its potential for growth and change, as well. "We are an authentic brand," he emphasizes. "The work we do here is for the love of the craft." This bone-deep dedication to the craft and the community, coupled with sound financial and business practices, has helped to ensure the long-term sustainability of Harrisville Designs in an industry where so many mills have closed or struggled to remain viable.

Nick provides a rare and valuable combination of a love and respect for the art and craft of using fiber to create, coupled with fresh ideas and new concepts that he is eager to explore.

He recently spearheaded the release of Nightshades, a line of ten Cormo yarns that are bale-dyed black and then tinted with existing HD colors. Black is, well, the black sheep of the yarn color family – it often gets little recognition or favor amongst knitters and weavers, even though we all recognize the importance that black plays as a foundational base in our wardrobes. "A very underserved demographic," as Nick calls it. One of the reasons for its lack of popularity is that it is very difficult to create a black yarn that doesn't appear flat or dull, making it photograph poorly. By introducing a hue of other colors to highlight the black, Nick has taken an accepted truism in the industry and turned it on its head. "Every once in a while," he says, "the knitting industry needs to be shaken up."

Throughout New England, there are examples of resurrection efforts being initiated in an attempt to protect and honor history, while becoming competitive in today's economy and planning for a sustainable future. Harrisville Designs excels at pairing these two concepts; for instance, it recently took a page out of history by working to revive the use of water power to mill some of its yarns. A portion of the proceeds from the sale of WATERshed and flyWHEEL yarns will be used to restore hydropower that originally powered the local mills. Harrisville Designs is showcasing the role that fiber arts plays in this resurrection journey, and the constant evolution of how fiber is made and used. The Colony family's generational story of the rescue of a mill, a town, and a local economy is an unparalleled example of the important role that textiles have played and can continue to play, well into the future.

Harrisville Designs

Website: harrisville.com

Address: 4 Mill Alley, Harrisville

Phone: 603.827.3996

Instagram: harrisvilledesigns

Harrisville Barn Jacket

by Andrea Hungerford

SIZING
Women's XXS (XS, S, M, M/L)(L, XL, XXL, XXXL)
Approx chest measurement 32(34, 36, 38, 40)(44, 48, 52, 58)"
Shown in Size M with approx ±8–10" ease

FINISHED MEASUREMENTS
Chest Circumference: 40.5 (42.75, 47, 49, 51.25)(55.5, 57, 61.25, 67.75)"
Back Length: 28 (29, 29, 29.5, 30)(30.25, 30.5, 31.5, 32)"

MATERIALS
Harrisville Designs WATERshed (100% Wool, 110 yds per 50 g), 13 (14, 15, 16, 17)(19, 19, 21, 23) skeins in Color Barn Door
US 8 (5 mm) 32" circular needles, stitch holder or waste yarn, tapestry needle
Four 1" buttons
Two ¾" buttons for pockets (optional)
20"×10" piece of fusible interfacing (optional)
½ yard of flannel fabric (optional)

GAUGE
15 sts and 28 rows = 4" in Seed Stitch with 1 strand WATERshed, blocked

NOTES
Barn jacket is worked in pieces from the bottom up in Seed Stitch with Garter Stitch trim and set-in sleeves. Button bands are worked on each front before seaming. Collar is picked up and worked after fronts and back are joined with a 3-needle bind-off. Optional flannel pocket flaps and sleeve cuffs are sewn on. This construction provides an opportunity to experiment with pairing knitwear and fabric. Use either hand or machine sewing to attach pocket flaps and cuffs.

STITCH PATTERN
Seed Stitch (worked over a multiple of 2 sts + 1)
All Rows: *K1, p1; rep from * to last st, k1.

DIRECTIONS
Back
Using long-tail cast-on method, CO 77 (81, 89, 93, 97)(105, 107, 115, 127) sts.
Work in Garter Stitch (knit all) for 1.75", ending with a RS row.
Next Row (WS): *K1, p1; rep from * to last st k1.

Cont working in Seed Stitch as established for 16 (16.75, 16.25, 16.75, 17)(17.25, 17.25, 18, 18)", or until piece measures 17.75 (18.5, 18, 18.5, 18.75)(19, 19, 19.75, 19.75)" or desired length from CO edge, ending on a WS row and keeping in mind that lengthening may require additional yarn.

Shape Armholes
BO 5 (5, 7, 7, 7)(7, 7, 9, 9) sts at beg of next two rows, then BO 1 st at the beg of next 4 (4, 6, 6, 6)(8, 6, 8, 16) rows. 63 (67, 69, 73, 77)(83, 87, 89, 93) sts.

Cont working in Seed Stitch until Back measures 9.25 (9.5, 10, 10, 10.25)(10.25, 10.5, 10.75, 11.25)" from armhole bind-off, ending a WS row.

Shape Shoulders
Row 1 (RS): Work 22 (23, 24, 26, 27)(30, 32, 32, 33) sts, pm, work to 4 sts before end of row, work GSR (*see Techniques on pg 93 for German Short Row*).
Row 2 (WS): Work in Seed Stitch as established to 3 (3, 4, 4, 4)(4, 5, 5, 5) sts before end of row, work GSR.
Row 3: Work to m, place these sts on holder for Right Shoulder, BO 19 (21, 21, 21, 23)(23, 23, 25, 27) sts, work to 3 (3, 4, 4, 4)(4, 5, 5, 5) sts before previous GSR, work GSR.

Shape Left Shoulder
Row 1 & all WS rows: Work in Seed Stitch to end of Row.
Row 2 (RS): BO 2 sts, work to 3 (3, 4, 4, 4)(4, 5, 5, 5) sts before previous GSR, work GSR.
Row 4: BO 1 st, work to 3 (3, 4, 4, 4)(4, 5, 5, 5) sts before previous GSR, work GSR.
Row 6: Work to end of row, working GSR ds tog. Break yarn and leave a tail 4 times the shoulder width to work 3-needle bind-off.

Shape Right Shoulder
Return held Right Shoulder sts to needle and join with WS facing.
Row 1 (WS): Work to 3 (3, 4, 4, 4)(4, 5, 5, 5) sts before previous GSR, work GSR.
Row 2 & all RS rows: Work in Seed Stitch to end of Row.
Row 3: BO 2 sts, work to 3 (3, 4, 4, 4)(4, 5, 5, 5) sts before previous GSR, work GSR.
Row 5: BO 1 st, work to 3 (3, 4, 4, 4)(4, 5, 5, 5) sts before previous GSR, work GSR.
Row 7: Work to end of row, working GSR ds tog. Break yarn and leave a tail 4 times the shoulder width to work 3-needle bind-off.

Right Front
Using long-tail cast-on method, CO 33 (35, 39, 41, 43)(47, 49, 53, 59) sts.
Work in Garter Stitch (knit all) for 1.75", ending with a RS row.
Next Row (WS): *K1, p1; rep from * to last st k1.

Cont working in Seed Stitch until Right Front measures the same as Back before armhole bind off, ending on a RS row.

Shape Armhole
BO 5 (5, 7, 7, 7)(7, 7, 9, 9) sts at beg of next row. Cont working in Seed Stitch as established and BO 1 st at the beg of next 2 (2, 3, 3, 3)(4, 3, 4, 8) WS rows. 33 (35, 39, 41, 43)(47, 49, 53, 59) sts.
Cont working in Seed Stitch until Right Front measures 8.25 (8.5, 9, 9, 9.25)(9.25, 9.5, 9.75, 10.25)" from armhole bind-off, ending with a WS row.

Shape Neck
BO 4 (5, 5, 5, 6)(6, 7, 8, 9) sts at beg of next row. Work 1 row as established. BO 1 st at beg of next 3 RS rows. 19 (20, 21, 23, 24)(27, 29, 29, 30) sts. If needed, cont working in Seed Stitch until Right Front measures 9.25 (9.5, 10, 10, 10.25)(10.25, 10.5, 10.75, 11.25)" from armhole bind-off, ending with a WS row.

Shoulder Shaping
Row 1 (RS): Work to 3 (3, 4, 4, 4)(4, 5, 5, 5) sts before end of row, work GSR.

Row 2 & all WS Rows: Work in Seed Stitch as established to end of row.
Row 3: Work to 3 (3, 4, 4, 4)(4, 5, 5, 5) sts before previous GSR, work GSR.
Rep last 2 rows 2 more times.
Next Row (RS): Work to end of row, working GSR ds tog. Break yarn.

Button Band

With RS facing and starting at hem, pick up approx 1 st for every 2 rows up front edge to neck bind-off.
Work in Garter Stitch (knit all) for 1".
Work buttonhole row (*see Techniques on pg 93*).
Cont in Garter Stitch until button band measures 2" from Right Front edge, ending with a RS row. BO all sts knitwise.

Left Front

Work as for Right Front until just before armhole shaping, ending on a WS row.

Shape Armhole

BO 5 (5, 7, 7, 7)(7, 7, 9, 9) sts at beg of next row. Cont working in Seed Stitch as established and BO 1 st at the beg of next 2 (2, 3, 3, 3)(4, 3, 4, 8) RS rows. 33 (35, 39, 41, 43)(47, 49, 53, 59) sts.
Cont working in Seed Stitch until Right Front measures 8.25 (8.5, 9, 9, 9.25)(9.25, 9.5, 9.75, 10.25)" from armhole bind-off, ending with a RS row.

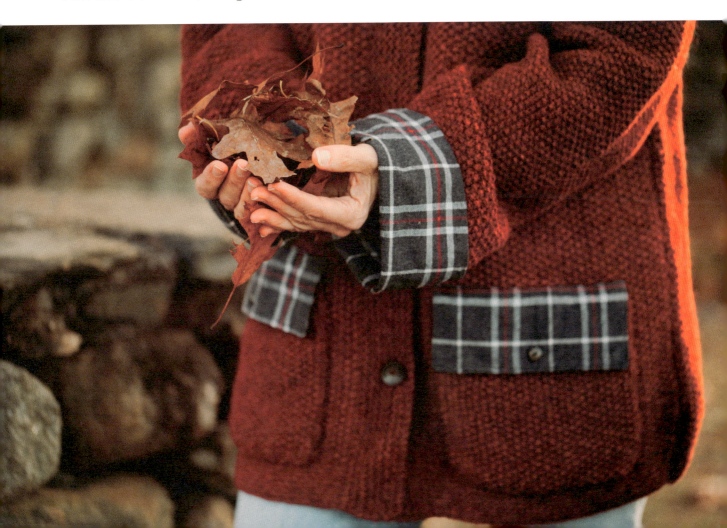

Shape Neck

BO 4 (5, 5, 5, 6)(6, 7, 8, 9) sts at beg of next row. Work 1 row as established. BO 1 st at beg of next 3 WS row. 19 (20, 21, 23, 24)(27, 29, 29, 30) sts. If needed, cont working in Seed Stitch until Right Front measures 9.25 (9.5, 10, 10, 10.25)(10.25, 10.5, 10.75, 11.25)" from armhole bind-off, ending with a RS row.

Shoulder Shaping

Row 1 (WS): Work to 3 (3, 4, 4, 4)(4, 5, 5, 5) sts before end of row, work GSR.
Row 2 & all RS Rows: Work in Seed Stitch as established to end of row.
Row 3: Work to 3 (3, 4, 4, 4)(4, 5, 5, 5) sts before previous GSR, work GSR.
Rep last 2 rows 2 more times.
Next Row (WS): Work to end of row, working GSR ds tog. Break yarn.

Button Band

With RS facing and starting at neck bind-off row, pick up approx 1 st for every 2 rows down front edge to hem.
Work in Garter Stitch (knit all) for 2", ending with a RS row.
BO all sts knitwise.

Sleeves

Make 2 the same.
CO 45 (47, 49, 51, 51)(53, 53, 55, 57) sts.

For knitted cuffs, start here:
Work in Garter Stitch for 3", ending with a RS row.
Next Row (WS): Purl.
Cont in Garter Stitch until sleeve measures 6" from CO edge, ending with a RS row.

If you'd like to create fabric cuffs instead, start here:
Next Row (WS): *K1, p1; rep from * to last st, k1.
Cont working Seed Stitch as established for 6 more rows.
Inc Row (RS): K1, m1, *p1, k1; rep from * to last 2 sts, p1, m1, k1. 2 sts inc'd.
Rep Inc Row every 10 rows 7 (8, 8, 9, 9)(9, 10, 11, 12) more times, incorporating new sts into Seed Stitch pattern while maintaining a 1-st Garter Stitch selvedge. 61 (65, 67, 71, 71)(73, 75, 79, 83) sts.
Cont working in Seed Stitch as established until Sleeve measures 14.75 (14.75, 15, 15, 15.5)(15.75, 15.75, 15.75, 15.75)" from CO edge (this includes 3" folded cuff (6" cuff total)).

Shape Sleeve Cap

BO 5 (5, 7, 8, 7)(7, 7, 9, 9) sts at the beg of next 2 rows, then BO 1 st at beg of next 18 (8, 18, 22, 22)(24, 26, 24, 26) rows.

Cont working in Seed Stitch as established, maintain 1-st Garter selvedge, and work Dec Row every RS row 2 (10, 0, 0, 1)(1, 1, 0, 0) times, then every other RS row 3 (2, 5, 5, 4)(4, 4, 6, 6) times. 23 (23, 23, 23, 25)(25, 25, 25, 27) sts.
Row 1 (RS): SSK, work in Seed Stitch as established to last 2 sts, k2tog. 2 sts dec'd.

BO 3 sts at beg of next 2 rows. BO 2 sts at beg of next 2 rows. BO rem 13 (13, 13, 13, 15)(15, 15, 15, 17) sts.

Pockets

Make 2.

CO 27 (27, 31, 31, 31)(31, 31, 31, 31) sts. Work in Seed Stitch until Pocket measures 6.5 (6.5, 7.5, 7.5)(7.5, 7.5, 7.5, 7.5)" from CO edge. BO all sts knitwise.

FINISHING

Block pieces to measurements.

Join shoulders using 3-needle bind-off.

Set in sleeves, then sew side and sleeve seams using Mattress Stitch. (If Garter Stitch cuff, fold cuff at St st. band, and tack in place.)

Using mattress stitch, sew pockets on. Center each pocket between the buttonband and the side seam, with the lower edge of the pocket right above the garter stitch hem.

Sew on buttons.

Collar

Starting at Right Front neck, at the middle of the button band, pick up and knit 15 (16, 16, 16, 17)(17, 18, 19, 20) sts up Right Front neck to shoulder, then pick up and knit 27 (29, 29, 29, 31)(31, 31, 33, 35) sts along back neck (1 st for each st BO plus 1 st in each shoulder seam), then pick up and knit 15 (16, 16, 16, 17)(17, 18, 19, 20) sts down the Left Front neck. 57 (61, 61, 61, 65)(65, 67, 71, 75) sts.

Row 1 (WS): Work in Seed Stitch.

Row 2 (RS): KFB, work in Seed st to last 2 sts, KFB, k1. 2 sts inc'd.

Short-row 1 (WS): Work in Seed Stitch for 32 (34, 34, 34, 36)(36, 37, 39, 41) sts, work GSR.

Short-row 2 (RS): Work in Seed Stitch for 6 sts, work GSR.

Short-row 3: Work in Seed Stitch to 5 sts past last GSR, working GSR ds tog, work GSR.

Rep last Short-row 3 more times.

Next Row (WS): Work in Seed St to end of Row, working GSR ds tog.

Turning Row (RS): KFB, Knit across, working GSR, to last 2 sts, KFB, k1.

Cont Collar as follows:

Rows 1–3 (WS): Work in Seed Stitch.

Row 4 (RS): KFB, work in Seed st to last 2 sts, KFB, k1. 2 sts inc'd.

Rep rows 1–4 until Collar measures 3.25" or desired length, measured at shoulder seam. BO knitwise.

FLANNEL POCKET FLAPS (optional)

Cut four pieces of flannel 3¾" × 7½ (7½ , 8½, 8½, 8½)(8½, 8½, 8½, 8½)" (or ½" wider than the width of the pocket).

Cut 2 pieces of interfacing the same size.

Iron the fusible interfacing on the WS of two of the pocket flaps.

Put one flap piece without interfacing and one flap piece with interfacing together, RS facing. Stitch around all four sides with a ¼" seam allowance, leaving a 2" gap in the middle of one of the long sides for turning. Clip corners, turn, push out the corners, and press. Fold in the raw edges of the gap and press in place.

Topstitch around all four sides 1/8" from the edge.

Repeat with second set of pocket flap pieces.

Pin one flap centered and ½" above the pocket opening. Stitch in place ¼" from the flap

18

edge, then again 1/8'' from the flap edge, backstitching at both ends. Create buttonholes in flaps and sew ¾'' buttons onto fronts of pockets (optional).

FABRIC CUFFS (optional)
From flannel fabric, cut two pieces 13'' wide × the circumference of the sleeve cuff + ½'' (for example, 16'' circumference + ½'' = 16 ½'' long).

Working one piece at a time and using a ¼'' seam allowance, stitch the shorter (13'') sides of one piece together, right sides facing, to form a tube. Press the seam open. Fold the tube in half in on itself, with wrong sides touching, so that it is now 6'' wide. Match up the center seam and the raw edges and press. Next, press the raw edges of each end ¼'' to the wrong side, to create a clean edge.

Slip the knit sleeve inside the fabric tube, with the raw edges of the tube positioned approximately ½'' from the end of the knit sleeve. Line up center seams of fabric tube and knit sleeve. Pin in place and stitch ¼'' from the edge of the fabric.

Unfold the cuff and press the seam allowance toward the sleeve opening. Topstitch on the fabric cuff 1/8'' from the seamline.

Fold the cuff in half and tack in place if desired.
Repeat with second cuff.

BODY   ## SLEEVE

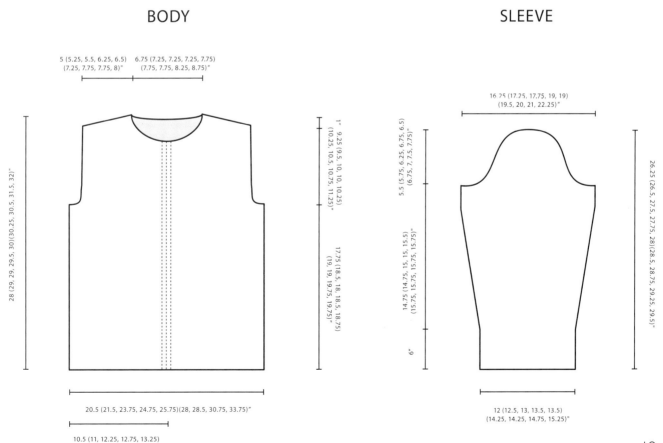

BODY

5 (5.25, 5.5, 6.25, 6.5)   6.75 (7.25, 7.25, 7.25, 7.75)
(7.25, 7.75, 7.75, 8)"   (7.75, 7.75, 8.25, 8.75)"

28 (29, 29, 29.5, 30)(30.25, 30.5, 31.5, 32)"

1" 9.25 (9.5, 10, 10, 10.25)
(10.25, 10.5, 10.75, 11.25)"

17.75 (18.5, 18, 18.5, 18.75)
(19, 19, 19.75, 19.75)"

20.5 (21.5, 23.75, 24.75, 25.75)(28, 28.5, 30.75, 33.75)"

10.5 (11, 12.25, 12.75, 13.25)
(14.25, 14.75, 15.75, 17.5)"

SLEEVE

16.25 (17.25, 17.75, 19, 19)
(19.5, 20, 21, 22.25)"

5.5 (5.75, 6.25, 6.75, 6.5)
(6.75, 7, 7.5, 7.75)"

26.25 (26.5, 27.5, 27.75, 28)(28.5, 28.75, 29.25, 29.5)"

14.75 (14.75, 15, 15, 15.5)
(15.75, 15.75, 15.75, 15.75)"

6"

12 (12.5, 13, 13.5, 13.5)
(14.25, 14.25, 14.75, 15.25)"

Fall color in the hills of Vermont (above), and along the shores of New Hampshire's Lake Winnipesaukee (below left and right).

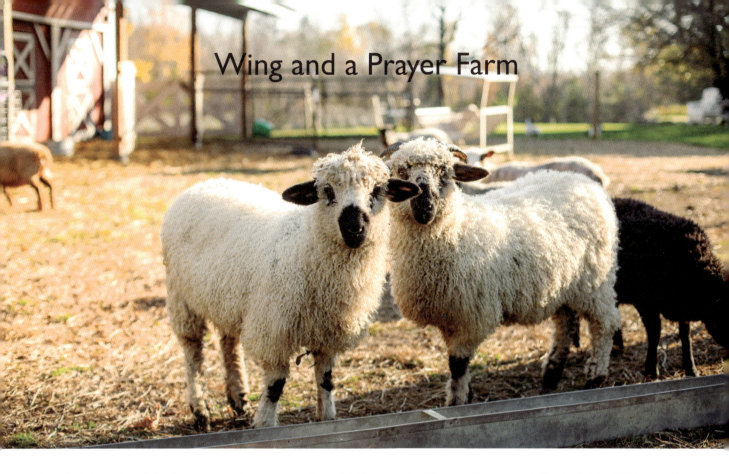

Wing and a Prayer Farm

It's a bright, crisp fall afternoon when we arrive at Wing and a Prayer Farm, past the height of Vermont's famous fall color, but with enough yellow and orange foliage to still make many of the trees glow. We're first greeted by the two resident farm dogs, followed closely by a rafter of turkeys (which, I learn, is the proper name for a group of the big birds). These are the friendliest turkeys I have ever encountered – a tom and his harem of hens escort us to the front porch of the farmhouse, gobbling conversationally along the way.

Before we reach the front door, Tammy White is off the porch and coming across the yard toward us. With her wide smile and infectious enthusiasm, Tammy is a warm and inviting host, and we immediately feel like part of the family as we cluster in her kitchen for a pie baking lesson. Tammy bakes hundreds of pies every year for customers who seek her out for her baking prowess and her delicious pies with the clever names: today we are baking "Pearway to Heaven," with pears from a neighbor that she swaps for one of Tammy's turkeys each year. As we bake, Tammy regales us with anecdotes about the farm, and it becomes clear why she has become such a powerful emissary for educating and sharing with people the life of a modern homesteader.

For 32 years, Tammy has lived on this farm in what she calls the South Shire of Vermont, where she's single-handedly raised three children and, with their help, transformed the land into a working farm. Every aspect of homesteading is present: livestock animals, vegetable and dye gardens, classes and workshops (titled the Farm and Home series), a pie baking business, Open Farm days, milling and naturally dyeing yarn from the resident fiber animals, and even creating and hosting the New England Fiber Arts Summit. Now visitors can even come for a farm stay through Airbnb, in a cottage that will "restore and reset your pace" with "comfortable, authentic farm coziness."

Tammy has deepened what started as a 4-H project into a lifestyle firmly rooted in Vermont's free spirit, but she has also thrown open her doors via modern technology, sharing and showing the daily life of the slow food and fiber movement with a wider audience. She uses the platform of Wing and a Prayer, via social media, to help spread the word about the importance of preserving small American farms, growing and milling domestic yarns, the science of natural dyeing, and a plethora of other homesteading activities and values. She makes all of these concepts accessible by using her ability to communicate in an easy, open manner to welcome people to the farm, both virtually and in person.

The reality of what Tammy has built over the years has not been easy, by any means. Many of the building blocks of the farm are a combination of hard work, partnerships with others, and luck or happenstance. For instance, the initial purchase of Valais Blacknose sheep – Wing and a Prayer's adorable emissaries, who can often be viewed on the farm's website "lambcam" – was actually a mistake, the result of an Internet auction gone horribly wrong. Tammy laughs as she tells the story of her naïve introduction into how easy it was to purchase sheep that lived all the way on the west coast via an online auction, even though she didn't actually intend to do so. But just as she has approached all of the challenges that the farm has thrown at her over the years, she rallied, conceived the idea of seeking sponsorships with local and farm-related businesses, and parlayed what could have been a terrible blow into something affirming and positive.

As we walk around the farm and Tammy introduces us to the animals, it becomes clear that they are the heart of Wing and a Prayer, and that they all hold a special place in her heart, as well. Unlike many farm animals, all of Tammy's creatures have been named, and she shares with us their origin stories, personalities, and funny anecdotes. In addition to 60 sheep representing over a half dozen breeds, there are angora goats, horses, donkeys, Maremma guardian dogs, barn cats and house cats, free-ranging turkeys and a gigantic coop full of every shape and color of chickens. The runner ducks are busy scrounging in the remnants of the vegetable garden, where they're guarded by Princess Peppermint the American Guinea Hog, who in addition to acting as a fierce protector, is also doing a remarkable job of keeping the weeds down between the vegetable beds and tilling up the soil. Tammy's deep attachment to the land and to every one of the animals she is responsible for showcases the best of farming and of those who choose such a difficult but important livelihood.

Tammy's daughter Char is busy harvesting the dye plants, bringing them in to hang dry from racks in a room off of the kitchen before the cold weather and the rains set in. She's in a hurry to finish, because the hay wagon will be arriving soon and the two of them will need

WELCOME ~onto~
Wing and a Prayer Farm
a breed-Specific fiber farm
☆☆ Fiber Producers ☆☆

THE DONKEYS
The mini donkeys are
adorable and friendly
livestock guard animals

Bilbo
Kalinha; Silver

Princess Peppermint
is an American Guinea Hog
aka the Governor

Ginger the Duck

Barn owl · Hoot ¥203

THE CHICKENS
Eggs, meat and parasite control
? please don't chase us!

THE SHEEP
Valais Blacknose
Shetland • Wensleydale
Cotswold • Merino • Cormo

THE ANGORA GOATS
'The Muppets' are
Mohair growers

THE ALPACAS
Produce soft fleece that is
warm, strong and water-resistant
+Also used as guard animals

THE CASHMERES
Soft   Smart
as a   as a
heck   whip

Fixing the World for the better,
one small farm
at a time w Tammy

THE HORSES
Ivy
i Nite Nite

THE DOGS

THE BARN CATS

WingandaPrayerFarm.com

to get all of the winter's hay off the wagon, onto the barn elevator, and up into the hayloft. "We can move them four bales at a time, and with 500 bales in all, it's a lot of work," Tammy laughs. As Char brings in armfuls of dye plants, Tammy talks about the importance of using what's available on the farm. "When I'm dyeing," she says, "I'm not striving to get the Pantone color of the year. I'm only getting what comes naturally out of the garden. It's means that we're not always competitive – sometimes the colors of my yarn aren't what is trendy in the marketplace that year. They just are what they are. My colors aren't repeatable because I'm working with whatever that year's harvest has brought. But it's a true and honest reflection of what the earth has produced in this time and place." Both the fiber and the color in all of Tammy's yarns embody this philosophy, and working with them feels like an opportunity to share in life on the farm.

In this and many other ways, Tammy sees her full-time job as an educator, a steward for the earth, and an advocate for the animals. The information she showcases illustrates how the decisions that fiber artists make in choosing their materials and supplies can influence the ability of a small farm like Wing and a Prayer to succeed. Tammy's ability to share with others her practice of heritage homesteading with modern values allows the impact and influence of Wing and a Prayer Farm to stretch far beyond this rural corner of Vermont, to a much broader community.

Wing and a Prayer Farm

Website: wingandaprayerfarm

Etsy: etsy.com/shop/wingandaprayerfarm

Instagram: wingandaprayerfarm

E-mail: hello@wingandaprayerfarm.com

Pearway to Heaven

double crust lattice pie by Tammy White of Wing and a Prayer Farm

When I was in middle school, we moved to Massachusetts to live near my grandmother. She made pies all the time and sold them at community events, and I was entranced by the smells coming out of her kitchen. Everyone knew and loved Grandma Brown's pies! I told my mother that I wanted to learn how to bake pies, and she told me to learn from Grandma Brown. My grandmother wouldn't give me the recipe; instead, she taught me by having me make pies alongside her.

Today, I make hundreds of pies each year for weddings, picnics, potlucks, and other events. Because I make 25-30 pies at a time for big events, I always make enough dough for four double-crusted pies (eight crusts) at a time. Pie dough freezes well, so whenever you need to make a pie, you can just pull out the remaining dough and your crust is ready to go!

INGREDIENTS

Crust:
5 cups flour
1 tablespoon sugar
1 teaspoon salt
14 ounces (5 cups) cold butter
2/3 cup ice cold water
One egg
1 tablespoon apple cider vinegar

Filling:
8 medium-size pears (you can add in a few apples, too)
¼ teaspoon vanilla bean paste or 1 teaspoon vanilla
½ teaspoon cinnamon
¾ cup raw cane sugar
3 tablespoons corn starch (4 tablespoons if fruit is very wet)
2 tablespoons crystalized ginger (optional)
1 tablespoon fresh ginger (grated)

DIRECTIONS

Crust:

1. Blend dry ingredients with a pastry blender. Cut butter in, a tablespoon at a time. It should be really cold, even frozen. Blend the butter in with a pastry blender until it makes pea-shaped bits, but don't over-work it.

2. Refrigerate at least 20 minutes, or up to overnight to let it rest.

3. Crack egg into 2/3 cup ice cold water. Add apple cider vinegar (you could also use lemon juice, or anything acidic). Whisk together, then add to the dry ingredients. Mix with your hands (move quickly so that you don't add too much heat from your hands).

4. Use your hands to form a roll – it may feel a little crumbly, but it will roll out after it rests. It should feel moist, like clay or playdough you just opened. Wrap the dough in Saran wrap or a plastic bag, using the plastic covering to manipulate it into the shape of a roll. By wrapping it, you can use the surface of the counter to work it into the shape you need, without getting your hands on it too much.

5. Refrigerate at least 30 minutes. Afterward, slice the roll into disks (divide it in half, then in half again, for a total of eight equally sized disks). You can cut the disks and wrap them individually, then remove from the freezer only what you need. When removing dough from the freezer, let it defrost for 20-30 minutes.

6. When rolling out the crust, the less you handle it, the better. Roll out only one way (instead of back and forth). Roll out to the size of your pie tin. Spray the bottom of the pie tin with nonstick spray. Fold the rolled out dough in half, then into fourths, lift it into the pie pan and unfold it.

Filling:
7. Peel pears (and apples, if you'd like to add in a few). Quarter the pear or apple, cut off any bad spots, then slice into long, thin slices ¼" thick.

8. Combine vanilla bean paste, cinnamon, crystalized ginger, sugar, and corn starch separately from the fruit. Mix fresh grated ginger in with the fruit, then add in dry ingredients. Spoon into the pie shell.

9. Form a lattice crust by rolling out the second crust, cutting it into strips, and then laying the strips down and weaving them one over, one under each other.

10. Brush the top crust with egg white.

11. Place the pie pan on parchment paper or a silpat before placing it into the oven, as it's likely to bubble over.

12. Bake for 75 minutes at 350 degrees. Makes one double-crust 9-inch pie

Alternatively, you can freeze the pie; work through Step 10, then wrap the unbaked pie and freeze.

Beyond the Maples

by Makenzie Alvarez

Embracing lovely classic stitches mixed with intertwining cables. Beyond the Maples showcases the beauty of each stitch, creating a unique and elegant design.

FINISHED MEASUREMENTS
Sizes Small (Large)
64 (72)" wingspan × 29.5 (33.5)" depth

MATERIALS
Wing & A Prayer Farm, The Happiest Yarn (100% US Wool [4 parts Shetland from Wing and a Prayer Farm, 1 part Romney from Doc Mason's Wool, 1 part Merino and spun from Battenkill Fibers] 150 yds per 57 g), 3(4) hanks each in Oatmeal (MC) and Natural (CC)
US 6 (4 mm) 32" circular needles, Size G crochet hook, 4 stitch markers, scrap yarn (for Garter Tab Cast On), cable needle, tapestry needle, row counter (optional)

GAUGE
20 sts and 36 rows = 4" in Garter Stitch, blocked

NOTES
Triangular shawl is worked starting from a garter tab cast on using two colors.

DIRECTIONS
Garter Tab Cast On
With crochet hook and scrap yarn, chain 5 sts. Slip your knitting needle into the back loops of 3 sts of the chain. With your working yarn, Knit 7 rows, do not turn. Next rotate work 90 degrees and pick up and knit 3 stitches on the Garter Tab Edge. Rotate your work 90 degrees again. Carefully undo the crochet chain and place the 3 stitches on Left Needle, and knit them. 9 sts.

Section 1
Note: This section will change colors every 2 rows. When switching colors overlap yarn to tuck one under another.
Set-up Row (WS): K3, pm, p1, pm, p1, pm, p1, pm, k3. 9 sts. Row 1 MC (RS): K3, sm, m1, k to marker, m1, sm, k1, sm, m1, k to marker, m1, sm, k3. 4 st inc'd; 13 sts.
Row 2 MC: K3, sm, k to marker, sm, p1, sm, k to marker, sm, k3.
Row 3 CC: K3, sm, m1, k to marker, m1, sm, k1, sm, m1, k to marker, m1, sm, k3. 4 st inc'd; 17 sts.
Row 4 CC: K3, sm, k to marker, sm, p1, sm, k to marker, sm, k3.
Rep Rows 1–4 twelve more times. 113 sts.

Section 2
Row 1 MC (RS): K3, sm, m1, k to marker, m1, sm, k1, sm, m1, k to marker, m1, sm, k3. 4 st inc; 117 sts.
Row 2 MC (WS): K3, sm, p to marker, sm, p1, sm, p1 to marker, sm, k3.
Rep Rows 1 and 2 ten more times. 157 sts.

Next Row 3 CC (RS): K3, sm, m1, k to marker, m1, sm, k1, sm, m1, k to marker, m1, sm, k3. 4 st inc; 161 sts.
Row 4 CC (WS): K3, sm, k to marker, sm, p1, sm, k to marker, sm, k3.
Rep Rows 1 and 2 eleven times. 205 sts.

Section 3 (worked in CC only)
Row 1 CC (RS): K3, sm, m1, k to marker, m1, sm, k1, sm, m1, k to marker, m1, sm, k3. 4 st inc'd; 209 sts.
Row 2 CC (WS): K3, sm, k to marker, sm, p1, sm, k to marker, sm, k3.
Row 3: K3, sm, m1, (p1, k1) rep to 1 st before marker, p1, m1, sm, k1, sm, m1, (p1, k1) rep to 1 st before marker, p1, m1, sm, k3. 4 sts inc'd; 213 sts.
Row 4: K3, sm, (p1, k1) rep to 1 st before marker, p1, sm, p1, sm, (p1, k1) rep to 1 st before marker, p1, sm, k3.
Rep Rows 3 and 4 eight (nine) more times. 245 (249) sts.
Rep Rows 1 and 2 once more. 249 (253) sts.

Section 4 (Large Size only)
Row 1 MC (RS): K3, sm, m1, k to marker, m1, sm, k1, sm, m1, k to marker, m1, sm, k3. 4 sts inc'd; 257 sts.
Row 2 MC (WS): K3, sm, p to marker, sm, p1, sm, p1 to marker, sm, k3.
Rep Rows 1 and 2 nine more times. 293 sts.
Row 3 CC: K3, sm, m1, k to marker, m1, sm, k1, sm, m1, k to marker, m1, sm, k3. 4 sts sinc'd; 297 sts.
Row 4 CC: K3, sm, k to marker, sm, p1, sm, k to marker, sm, k3.

All Sizes
Row 1 MC (RS): K3, sm, m1, k to marker, m1, sm, k1, sm, m1, k to marker, m1, sm, k3. 4 st inc'd; 253 (301) sts.
Row 2 MC (WS): K3, sm, p to marker, sm, p1, sm, p1 to marker, sm, k3.
Rep Rows 1 and 2 seven more times. 281 (329) sts.
Row 3 CC: K3, sm, m1, k to marker, m1, sm, k1, sm, m1, k to marker, m1, sm, k3. 4 sts inc'd; 285 (333) sts.
Row 4 CC: K3, sm, k to marker, sm, p1, sm, k to marker, sm, k3.
Rep Rows 1 and 2 six times. 309 (357) sts.
Rep Rows 3 and 4 once. 313 (361) sts.
Rep Rows 1 and 2 four times. 329 (377) sts.
Rep Rows 3 and 4 once. 333 (381) sts.
Rep Rows 1 and 2 two times. 341 (389) sts.
Rep Rows 3 and 4 once. 345 (393) sts.
Rep Rows 1 and 2 once. 349 (397) sts.
Rep Rows 3 and 4 once. 353 (401) sts.

Section 5 (worked in CC only)
Work Rows 1–30 following instructions as follows (Right and Left Side pattern repeats

between increases are shown in the Chart):

Row 1 CC (RS): K3, sm, m1, (p2, k2) 43 (49) times, p1, m1p, sm, k1, sm, m1p, p1, (k2, p2) 43 (49) times, m1, sm, k3. 357 (405) sts.

Row 2 and all WS CC: Work in established pattern.

Row 3: K3, sm, m1p, k1, (p2, k2) 43 (49) times, p2, m1, sm, k1, sm, m1, (p2, k2) 43 (49) times, p2, k1, m1p, sm, k3. 361 (409) sts.

Row 5: K3, sm, m1, p1, k1, (p2, 1/1 LC) 43 (49) times, p2, k1, m1p, sm, k1, sm, m1p, k1, (p2, 1/1 RC) 43 (49) times, p2, k1, p1, m1, sm, k3. 365 (413) sts.

Row 7: K3, sm, m1p, k1, p1, (1/1 LPC, 1/1 RPC) 44 (50) times, p1, m1, sm, k1, sm, m1, p1, (1/1 LPC, 1/1 RPC) 44 (50) times, p1, k1, m1p, sm, k3. 369 (417) sts.

Row 9: K3, sm, m1, p1, k1, (p2, 1/1 RC) 44 (50) times, p2, k1, m1p, sm, k1, sm, m1p, k1, (p2, 1/1 LC) 44 (50) times, p2, k1, p1, m1, sm, k3. 373 (421) sts.

Row 11: K3, sm, m1, k1, p1, (1/1 LPC, 1/1 RPC) 45 (51) times, p1, m1, sm, k1, sm, m1, p1, (1/1 LPC, 1/1 RPC) 45 (51) times, p1, k1, m1, sm, k3. 377 (425) sts.

Row 13: K3, sm, m1p, k2, (p2, 1/1 LC) 45 (51) times, p2, k1, m1, sm, k1, sm, m1, k1, (p2, 1/1 RC) 45 (51) times, p2, k2, m1p, sm, k3. 381 (429) sts.

Row 15: K3, sm, m1p, p1, (k2, p2) 46 (52) times, k2, m1p, sm, k1, sm, m1p, (k2, p2) 46 (52) times, k2, p1, m1p, sm, k3. 385 (433) sts.

Row 17: K3, sm, m1, (p2, k2) 47 (53) times, p1, m1, sm, k1, sm, m1, p1, (k2, p2) 47 (53) times, m1, sm, k3. 389 (437) sts.

Row 19: K3, sm, m1p, k1, (p2, 1/1 LC) 47 (53) times, p1, k1, m1p, sm, k1, sm, m1p, k1, p1, (1/1 RC, p2) 47 (53) times, k1, m1p, sm, k3. 393 (441) sts.

Row 21: K3, sm, m1, p1, (1/1 LPC, 1/1 RPC) 47 (53) times, 1/1 LPC, k1, p1, m1, sm, k1, sm, m1, p1, k1, (1/1 RPC, 1/1 LPC) 47 (53) times, 1/1 RPC, p1, m1, sm, k3. 397 (445) sts.

Row 23: K3, sm, m1p, k1, (p2, 1/1 RC) 48 (54) times, p1, k1, m1p, sm, k1, sm, m1p, k1, p1, (1/1 LC, p2) 48 (54) times, k1, m1p, sm, k3. 401 (449) sts.

Row 25: K3, sm, m1, p1, (1/1 LPC, 1/1 RPC) 48 (54) times, 1/1 LPC, k1, p1, m1p, sm, k1, sm, m1p, p1, k1, (1/1 RPC, 1/1 LPC) 48 (54) times, 1/1 RPC, p1, m1, sm, k3. 405 (453) sts.

Row 27: K3, sm, m1, k1, (p2, 1/1 LC) 49 (55) times, p2, m1, sm, k1, sm, m1, (p2, 1/1 RC) 49 (55) times, p2, k1, m1, sm, k3. 409 (457) sts.

Row 29: K3, sm, m1p, (k2, p2) 50 (56) times, k1, m1, sm, k1, sm, m1, k1, (p2, k2) 50 (56) times, m1p. 413 (461) sts.

Row 30: Worked in established pattern.

FINISHING
BO all sts. Wet block; allow to dry completely.

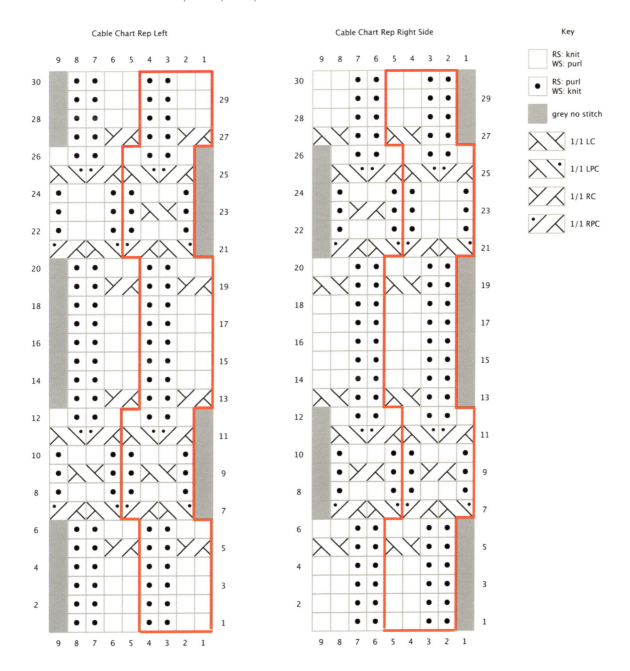

Alice Ogden Black Ash Baskets

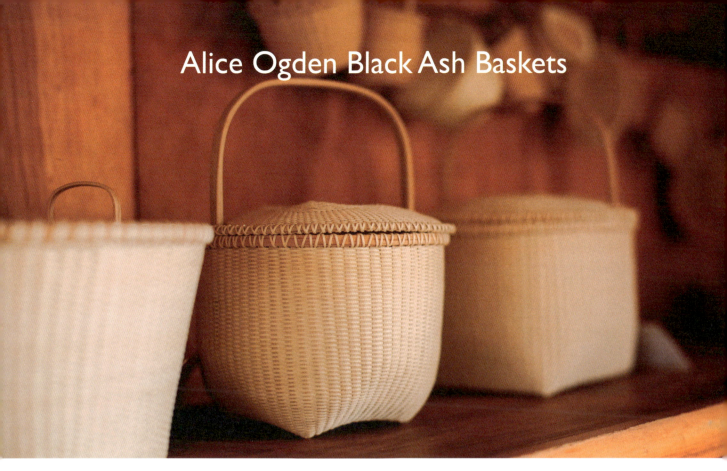

Shaker black ash baskets are rooted in traditions that span over 200 years, dating back to the 18th century. The Shakers were a splinter sect of Quakers formed in England, and later in the American colonies, known for their simple lifestyles, pacifist and religious beliefs, and the beautiful furniture and crafts that they created. It is believed that Shakers began weaving their own baskets when those they had purchased from local Native Americans weren't durable enough to withstand the heavy usage of daily agricultural work. Originally, basketmaking was a task shared between the brethren and sisters; the brethren cut and prepared the raw materials, and the sisters did the majority of the weaving. Wooden molds were used to ensure uniformity and perfection in each piece. However, the decline of Shaker men in the mid-19th century meant that the sisters took over a majority of the basketmaking work, and as a result, the designs were feminized and "fancy-work" baskets were created.

Baskets were made for day-to-day living, so many were designed for specific purposes, or even as units of measurement: bushel, half bushel, peck, and half peck were once standard sizes. Large baskets were constructed for heavy produce such as apples, potatoes, and squash. Smaller baskets were used for berry picking, flowers, or personal items.

Because ash wood is soft and splits easily, it's not useful for furniture making, but it is uniquely suited for basket making. The Shakers would harvest the ash trees and then pound steadily along the log to loosen the growth rings, which separated into even layers called splints. These layers were split again to get the desired thickness, then the strips were cut to a desired and consistent width. While other materials were sometimes woven in for decorative effect, ash remained the primary construction material for Shaker baskets. Finally, the rims and handles were carved from the same piece of wood and lashed to the basket with the same splints used for weaving.

Alice Ogden has continued the tradition of Shaker basketmaking for the past 40 years. The roots of this tradition run in the family; Alice's mother was a chair caner, her husband is a professional logger, and harvesting the logs is a family affair. Ash trees grow in swampy areas, so it isn't feasible to use a tractor. Instead, Alice and her family put on tall boots and use log cant hooks and strong backs to manually pull out the felled logs.

Alice peels the bark off the logs with a draw knife, then she uses a wooden mallet to pound the length of the log until the layers of wood separate at the growth rings. Once the splints are sorted, split again until smooth, and cut into consistent widths, Alice uses wooden forms and begins weaving. She uses the traditional one over, one under pattern for most of the baskets, although cheese baskets are woven in an open hexagonal weave. These baskets were originally used to drain the cheese curds and separate them from the whey, and the open weave pattern gives the wet wooden splints room to swell.

The final step in the process is using a shave horse to whittle the rim and handles out of white oak, and then lash them in place to the top edge of the basket. Alice's use of this traditional method makes her baskets unique, even among other handmade basket weavers. All of this hand work is extremely time-intensive, but Alice notes that "as an artist, making my materials from scratch gives me complete control over the quality that I put out."

Because of the investment of time and effort required for each basket, and the number of different options for the basket's size and shape, Alice's customers place pre-orders and then she makes each basket to order. She also weaves miniature Christmas ornaments – a different style each year – and some of her customers have been collecting them for years (there are 22 in all now). And several times a year, Alice will teach workshops; over the course of two full days and using kits that Alice has prepared, her students will learn all of the steps necessary to complete a single basket.

The draw of Alice's work is not only the beauty of its simple, traditional patterns and processes, but its functionality, as well. Long before the ease of cardboard boxes and plastic containers, baskets held great value for the tasks of everyday life. Each basket had a specific purpose that was integral to its owner's daily routine. This integration of craftsmanship, beauty, and functionality remains as relevant today as ever – perhaps even more so, in an age when the challenge is to confront and reject the easy disposibility of much of the items that we use on a day-to-day basis throughout our lives.

Alice Ogden Black Ash Baskets

Website: aliceogden.com

E-mail: alice@aliceogden.com

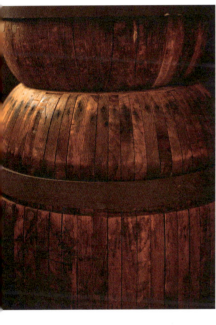

The top of Mt. Washington peaks above the clouds (above left). Views of Omni Mount Washington, one of New Hampshire's oldest and grandest resorts (upper right and below).

Odacier Knitting and Sewing Patterns

Creating with fiber and fabric is in Ellen Mason's blood: her grandmother, mother, and sisters all sewed and knitted, and Ellen has been making her own clothes since she was a little girl. "I would go to bed with pattern books," she recollects. "In high school, I was the only kid taking private weaving and knitting machine lessons." Ellen's parents encouraged and supported her endeavors; in fact, the knitting machine was a 16th birthday present, and the heirloom wooden loom that now sits in Ellen's bedroom was built by her father.

Throughout her life, Ellen has focused her making on what is comfortable and wearable, and this has shaped the philosophy that underlies her knitting and sewing patterns. "I love simple stockinette," she smiles. "Early in my knitting career, I knit lots of lace, but I never wear those sweaters. The thing I tend to grab for over and over is the plainest, most basic sweater I have. Why not embrace and elevate that simplicity?"

Ellen's sewing patterns echo this philosophy by emphasizing simple shapes and easy-to-fit, easy-to-wear garments. Whenever she designs a sewing pattern, Ellen thinks about the sewists who will be bringing it to life. "I want the sewing experience to be fun. I want them to feel like they've climbed a rung of the ladder when they're done." To that end, one hallmark of her patterns is a multitude of clearly marked diagrams, helpful hints, and thoroughly written directions. Much of Ellen's work reflects her belief in teaching others and helping them to embrace learning and growth. "We need to allow ourselves to be beginners," she explains. "We expect success too quickly. It's not pretty in the beginning, but we don't allow ourselves that ugly phase as adults. We just expect to learn something new without any failures or growing pains."

Every detail of Ellen's patterns is thoughtful and reflective of her warm personality and sense of humor. There is significance in the little touches, like the pattern names - which honor significant people in her life - and the cover art for each of the patterns, sketched by Ellen herself as happy cartoons. The business is named Odacier after her grandmother's first name, and Ellen's own middle name. And, although she doesn't have any formal patternmaking training, Ellen credits her love of math with giving her the gumption to tackle learning how to do her own grading, schematics, diagrams, and patternmaking.

Doc Mason Wool is another outgrowth of Ellen's belief in collaboration and building community. The story begins with her brother-in-law "Doc Mason," a local veterinarian who lives on a farm and specializes in training and rehabilitating herding dogs. The dogs start their training by herding ducks, but Doc Mason eventually acquired a flock of sheep to advance the dogs' skills. The sheep are primarily Clun Forest, but there are many other breeds scattered amongst the flock, as well. With so many sheep and nothing to do with the wool, Doc Mason began taking the fleece to a small woolen mill on

Prince Edward Island. One year, as Ellen tells it, the mill wove blankets from the wool, and her husband and his eight siblings each received one for Christmas. While the blankets were not popular amongst the recipients because they were rough and scratchy, Ellen was touched and inspired. So when Doc Mason asked her if she would be interested in using the yarn, she jumped at the opportunity. Since then, she has worked directly with the mill to turn Doc Mason Wool into a yarn that is softer to the touch, yet still rustic and authentic to its roots.

Odacier

Designer: Ellen Mason

Website: odacier.com

Etsy: etsy.com/shop/Odacier?ref=ss_profile

Instagram: odacier

Sarah Ann Tunic

by Ellen Mason

The Sarah Ann Tunic is a boxy top with a shallow V-neck secured by visible hand stitching. The sleeves feature dropped shoulders, a subtle gather at the top, and elastic cuffs. They can be made bracelet length or three-quarter length. Choose a hem that suits your needs: hip length for unmindful tucking into a belted skirt, or tunic length to pair with leggings or skinny jeans. Add a pocket or two for keeping your day's treasures.

Follow this link to download pattern and instructions: https://www.byhandserial.com/sarah-anne-tunic-instructions

FABRIC SUGGESTIONS
Light to midweight woven fabric such as linen, rayon, chambray, double gauze, flannel, or homespun cotton.

SUPPLIES
Prewashed fabric (yardage requirements on following page)
Matching thread
24 inches of ¾-inch wide elastic
Sharp fabric shears
Tailor's chalk or your preferred marking pen/pencil
Straight pins
Embroidery thread or Sashiko thread (optional)
Embroidery needle

YARDAGE REQUIREMENTS

	XS	S	M	L	XL	2XL	3XL
TUNIC							
Long Sleeve							
44"	2 3/4	2 3/4	2 7/8	3	3 3/8	3 1/2	3 5/8
54"	1 5/8	1 5/8	1 5/8	1 3/4	2 3/4	2 7/8	2 7/8
Short Sleeve							
44"	2 5/8	2 3/4	2 3/4	2 7/8	3 1/4	3 3/8	3 1/2
54"	1 1/2	1 1/2	1 1/2	1 5/8	2 5/8	2 3/4	2 3/4
SHIRT							
Long Sleeve							
44"	2 1/4	2 3/8	2 3/8	2 1/2	2 7/8	3	3 1/8
54"	1 3/8	1 3/8	1 3/8	1 1/2	2 1/4	2 3/8	2 1/2
Short Sleeve							
44"	2 1/8	2 1/4	2 1/4	2 3/8	2 7/8	2 7/8	3
54"	1 1/4	1 1/4	1 1/4	1 3/8	2 1/8	2 1/4	2 3/8

If your bust or belly measures:	30-32 in.	33-35 in.	36-38 in.	39-42 in.	43-46 in.	47-50 in.	51-54 in.
Try this size:	**XS**	**S**	**M**	**L**	**XL**	**2XL**	**3XL**
SARAH ANN TUNIC FINISHED MEASUREMENTS in inches							
A Bust	37 1/4	40 3/8	43 3/8	47 1/4	51 1/8	55 1/8	59
B Hips	38 3/4	41 7/8	45	49 1/8	53 1/8	57 1/4	61 1/4
C Upper arm	14 1/4	15 1/2	16 5/8	18 1/8	19 5/8	21 1/8	22 5/8
D Neckline to cuff, short sleeve	19 1/2	20 3/8	21 1/4	22 3/8	23 5/8	24 3/4	26
E Neckline to cuff, long sleeve	23 3/8	24 1/8	25	26 1/4	27 3/8	28 5/8	29 3/4
F Neckline width	7 1/8	7 5/8	8 1/8	8 1/2	9	9 1/2	10
G Neckline depth	5 1/2	6	6 3/8	7	7 5/8	8 1/8	8 3/4
H Shirt: Shoulder to front hem	22 1/2	23 1/4	24 1/8	25 1/4	26 3/8	27 1/2	28 5/8
I Tunic: Shoulder to front hem	29 7/8	30 5/8	31 1/2	32 5/8	33 3/4	34 7/8	36

FABRIC SUGGESTIONS

Light to midweight woven fabric such as linen, rayon, chambray, double gauze, flannel, or homespun cotton.

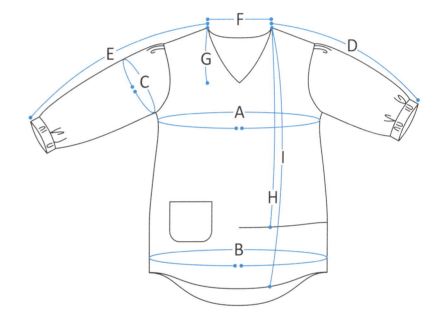

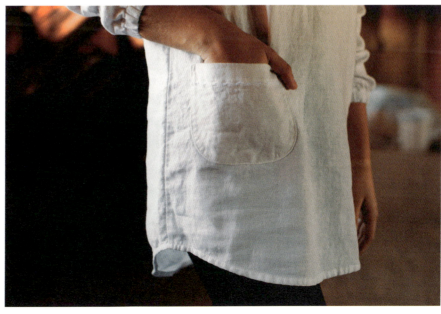

There are innumerable streams, woodlands, and small farms to explore in Vermont and New Hampshire, and the quality of the autumn light makes them beautiful to photograph.

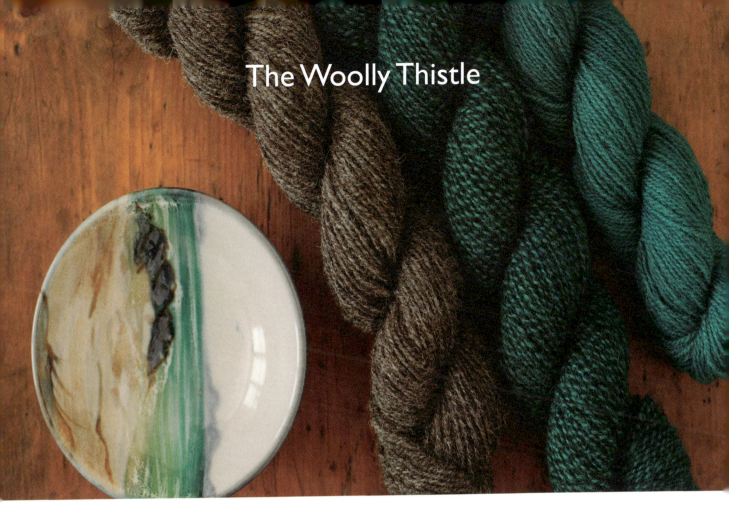

The Woolly Thistle

Fiber enthusiasts choose their artistic medium – yarn – not only for its color, weight, and texture, but for its origin story, as well. Knitting, crocheting, or weaving with yarn from other countries allows makers to travel through their yarn by touching a little bit of those far-away places. Many fiber artists dream of traveling to Scotland or England, and working with British yarns, in their dusky, heathered colors, crunchy wooliness, sturdy warmth, and depth of texture, conjure up the foggy moors of England or the windswept isles of Scotland. Small-batch UK yarns often use single-breed wool from British sheep, many of which are not found anywhere else in the world. For instance, Armscote Manor Yarns, which originate from an 18th century manor house, is working to bring back the oldest sheep breed in England.

Even the color names often reflect their origin. The Border Mill's Shetland yarn is inspired by Scotland's far north coast, and the colors include Loch Maree, Isle of Ewe, and Knockan Crag. Using these yarns gives makers a chance to support small artisan farms and mills that, although geographically far away, are part of a close-knit fiber community in the United States and around the world.

Knitters may hesitate to experiment with British yarns because of the potential difficulty in obtaining them. Currency conversions, shipping costs, and the lengthy wait to receive orders are all deterrents to ordering yarn from halfway around the world. This is where Corinne Tomlinson comes in. For Corinne, a Scottish native, these places are home. "These are places that I know. My mom lived in Fair Isle for the last couple of years, and I took my kids there on vacation. I used to go to the Outer Hebrides, off the coast of Scotland, for summer holidays. These are beautiful, picturesque, dreamy places."

The Woolly Thistle

Owner: Corinne Tomlinson

Website:
thewoollythistle.com

Instagram:
thewoollythistle

Corinne conceived of The Woolly Thistle, a stateside online yarn shop, as a way to source and provide British and Scottish yarns to customers in the United States. Once considered too scratchy, many of these yarns are now receiving the love they deserve. Corinne is drawn by the tactile nature of the British wools. "Once you get over the idea that it's 'scratchy', you realize that it's really pebbly, textured, warm, woolen spun wool. I feel like as knitters we have moved into wanting real wool, which leads to real knitting of classic, timeless, heirloom quality work. The pieces get better with time." There are a multitude of uses for these yarns: woolly sweaters and outer garments that keep their wearers warm and dry, lacy and delicate traditional haps, and colorwork that creates the impression of painting with watercolors.

The Woolly Thistle stocks an enviable variety of UK yarns, including mainstays like Erika Knight and John Arbon; Ulst, which is spun in a mill on an island in the Outer Hebrides of Scotland; many different lines of Blacker; Little Grey Sheep's Hampshire yarns; a dizzying array of colors from Jamieson & Smith; and West Yorkshire Spinners, which is "reared, sheared, and spun in Britain." Corinne has expanded her stock to include several European yarns, as well, including Tukuwool from Finland and Rauma yarns from Norway.

In addition to yarn, Corinne offers a beautiful array of British and Scottish notions and accessories. Hand-turned wooden yarn bowls from Northumbria are available in sycamore, spalted beech, oak, cherry, and ash. Highland Stoneware notions dishes from Scotland are designed with handpainted sheep, thistle, or landscapes. Katie Green tea towels feature illustrations of all 72 British sheep breeds. The shop also includes a carefully curated selection of books, many showcasing Fair Isle patterns and colorwork. On the day we visited, large piles of freshly printed 2019 Shetland Wool Week books were waiting to be shipped out.

Future plans for The Woolly Thistle include the continuation of Corinne's podcast, a new YouTube channel, and the possibility of a retail store. "I want to continue to grow, serve more customers, and get the word out that woolly wool is knitting for a lifetime," Corinne smiles. "It will last forever."

Spruce Peak Pullover

by Amy Christoffers

FINISHED MEASUREMENTS
Chest Circumference: 37 (41, 46, 50, 54)(59, 63, 68, 72)"
Back Length at Center Back: 22 (22.75, 23.5, 23.75, 24.25) (24.75, 25.25, 25.75, 26.25)

MATERIALS
Green Mountain Spinnery (100% Wool, 180 yds per 57 g), 5 (6, 7, 7, 8)(9, 10, 11, 12) skeins in Evergreen US 8 (5 mm) for body and sleeves, US 6 (4 mm) needles for ribbing (circular and DPN), tools/notions: 2 stitch markers, spare needle for 3-needle bind off (or use the DPN for the sleeves), tapestry needle for weaving in ends.

GAUGE
19 sts and 24 rows = 4" in St st, blocked
10 stitch lace repeat =2.25" after blocking

NOTES
This pullover is intended to be worn with a relaxed fit—not too loose, not too tight but just right. Suggested ease is a very personal thing. The best way to choose a size is to measure an article of clothing that has the desired fit—in this case I'd suggest a comfy sweatshirt. Measure the garment armpit to armpit and select the size in the pattern that matches most closely. This could be anywhere from 2-12" above the actual chest measurement, depending on your personal style.

It is easy to customize this garment to your preferred length—just plan ahead and purchase yarn accordingly if you plan to add additional length.

STITCH PATTERN
Worked in the round:
Rnds 1, 3, 5 & 7: K1, yo, k3, cdd, k3, yo.
Rnds 2, 4, 6 * 8: K1, p9.
Rnd 9: K2, yo, k2, cdd, k2, yo, k1.
Rnd 10: K2, p7, k1.
Rnd 11: K3, yo, k1, cdd, k1, yo, k2.
Rnd 12: K3, p5, k2.
Rnd 13: K4, yo, cdd, yo, k3.
Rnds 14, 15, & 16: Knit.

Worked back and forth in rows:
Rows 1, 3, 5 & 7: K1, yo, k3, cdd, k3, yo,
Rows 2, 4, 6 & 8: K9, p1.
Row 9: K2, yo, k2, cdd, k2, yo, k1.
Row 10: P1, k7, p2.
Row 11: K3, yo, k1, cdd, k1, yo, k2.
Row 12: P2, k5, p3.
Row 13: K4, yo, cdd, yo, k3.
Rows 14 & 16: Purl.
Row 15: Knit.

DIRECTIONS

Body

With smaller circular needles, CO 164 (184, 204, 224, 244) (264, 284, 304, 324) sts, place marker and join for working in the round.

Set up Rib: [k1, p1] to end. Work in rib as established for 17 more rnds. Change to larger circular needle.

Next round: K82 (92, 102, 112, 122) (132, 142, 152, 162) sts, pm for side, k to end.

Set up pattern: K1, work the 10 stitch chart repeat 8 (9, 10, 11, 12) (13, 14, 15, 16) times, k1, sm, k1 work the 10-stitch chart repeat 8 (9, 10, 11, 12) (13, 14, 15, 16) times, k1.

Work as established repeating the chart/pattern rnds 1–16 until piece measures 14" ending with an odd pattern rnd.

From this point continue working in pattern back and forth in rows.

Back

Turn work.

Using the backwards loop method, CO 1 stitch, p1, then work next (even pattern row) to side marker, turn, place sts for front on a spare needle if desired. Work the CO stitch in St st (knit on RS, purl on WS). 83 (93, 103, 113, 123) (133, 143, 153, 163) sts on the needle.

Continue working in pattern as established, until back measures 6 (7.5, 8, 8, 8.25)(8.5, 8.75, 9, 9.25)" (or to desired armhole depth) from the dividing row, ending with a WS row. After completing 7 (7, 7, 7, 7) (8, 8, 8, 8) total repeats of the pattern, continue work in St st.

Shape Shoulders

Short row 1 (RS): Work to 7 sts before the end of the row, w&t.
Short row 2 (WS): Work to 7 sts before the end of the row, w&t.
Short row 3 (RS): Work to 5 sts before the w&t, w&t.
Short row 4 (WS): Work to 5 sts before the w&t, w&t.

Repeat last 2 short rows 2 (3, 4, 5, 6) (7, 8, 9, 10) times more.
Next row: Work to end, picking up the wraps and working them together with their sts.
Next row: Work to end, picking up the wraps and working them together with their sts.
Break yarn, place live sts on a holder for 3-needle BO.

Front

Rejoin yarn to the WS. Using the backwards loop method, CO 1 stitch, p1, then work next (even pattern row) to side marker, turn, place sts for front on a spare needle if desired. Work the CO stitch in St st (knit on RS, purl on WS). 83 (93, 103, 113, 123) (133, 143, 153, 163) sts on the needle.

Continue working in pattern as established, when there is until Front measures 5 (5.5, 6, 6, 6.5)(7, 7.5, 7.5, 8)" from the dividing row.

Shape Neck

Next row: Work in pattern over 36 (41, 46, 51, 56)(61, 66, 71, 76) sts, BO the next 11, work 36 (41, 46, 51, 56)(61, 66, 71, 76) sts to end.

Right Shoulder

Work 1 WS row.
Next row: BO 4 sts, work to end.
Work 1 WS row.
Next row: BO 3 sts, work to end.
Work 1 WS row.
Next row: BO 2 sts, work to end.
Work 1 WS row.
Next row: BO 1 st, work to end.
Work 1 WS row.

Repeat the last 2 rows 3 times more—23 (28, 33, 38, 43)(48, 53, 58, 63) sts remain.

Work even until Right front measures 6 (7.5, 8, 8, 8.25)(8.5, 8.75, 9, 9.25) from the dividing row, ending with an even (WS) row (or to desired armhole depth). After completing 7 (7, 7, 7, 7)(8, 8, 8, 8) repeats of the pattern continue to work in St st.

Shape Shoulders

Short row 1 (RS): Work to 7 sts before the end of the row, w&t.
Work 1 WS row.
Short row 3 (RS): Work to 5 sts before the w&t, w&t.
Work 1 WS row.

Repeat the last 2 rows 2 (3, 4, 5, 6)(7, 8, 9, 10) times more.
Next row: Work to end, picking up the wraps and working them together with their sts.
Work 1 WS row.
Break yarn, place live sts on a holder for 3-needle BO.

Left Shoulder

Rejoin yarn to WS, BO 4 sts, work to end.
Work 1 RS row.
Next row: BO 3 sts, work to end.
Work 1 RS row.
Next row: BO 2 sts, work to end.
Work 1 RS row.
Next row: BO 1 st, work to end.
Work 1 RS row.

Repeat the last 2 rows 3 times more—23 (28, 33, 38, 43)(48, 53, 58, 63) sts remain.

Work even until Left front measures 6 (7.5, 8, 8, 8.25)(8.5, 8.75, 9, 9.25) from the dividing row, ending with an odd (RS) row (or to desired armhole depth). After completing 7 (7, 7, 7, 7)(8, 8, 8, 8) row/round repeats of the pattern continue to work in St st.

Shape Shoulders

Short row 1 (WS): Work to 7 sts before the end of the row, w&t.
Work 1 RS row.
Short row 3 (WS): Work to 5 sts before the w&t, w&t.
Work 1 RS row.

Repeat the last 2 rows 2 (3, 4, 5, 6)(7, 8, 9, 10) times more.
Next row: Work to end, picking up the wraps and working them together with their sts.

Turn work so that the WS is facing out, return held sts to needles, join shoulders and BO: Work 3-needle BO over the 23 (28, 33, 38, 43)(48, 53, 58, 63) left front and back sts, BO 37 back neck sts, work 3-needle BO over the 23 (28, 33, 38, 43)(48, 53, 58, 63) right front and back sts to end. Break yarn.

Turn work RS out again.

Sleeves
With larger needles, pick up and knit 64 (68, 74, 74, 76)(80, 84, 84, 88) sts at armhole opening, starting at the underarm. Divide sts evenly over 3 DPN (or use your preferred method for working a small circumference), pm and join for working in the round. Work in St st for 9 (9, 7, 7, 7)(7, 7, 6, 6) rnds.

Shape Sleeves
Decrease round: K1, k2tog, knit to the last 2 sts, ssk—2 sts dec'd.

Repeat the decrease round every 10 (10, 8, 8, 8)(6, 6, 6, 6) rnds 6 (6, 8, 8, 8)(11, 11, 11, 11) times more—50 (54, 56, 56, 58)(56, 60, 60, 64) sts remain. Work even in St st until sleeve measures 14.5" or 2.5" less then desired sleeve length.

Change to smaller DPN.
Set up Rib: [k1, p1] repeat to end. Work in rib as established for 17 more rnds. BO in rib.

FINISHING
Neck band: Pick up and knit 84–90 sts evenly around the neck opening.
Set up Rib: [k1, p1] repeat to end. Work in rib as established for 5 more rnds. BO in rib.

Weave in ends. Block as desired.

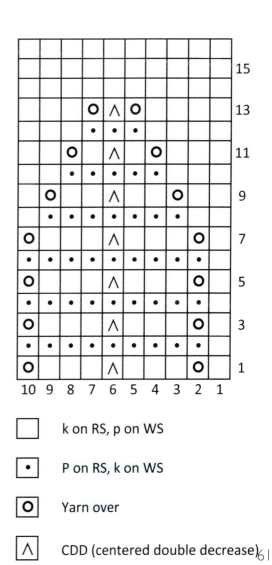

										15
			O	∧	O					13
			•	•	•					
		O		∧		O				11
		•	•	•	•	•				
	O			∧			O			9
	•	•	•	•	•	•	•			
O				∧				O		7
•	•	•	•	•	•	•	•	•		
O				∧				O		5
•	•	•	•	•	•	•	•	•		
O				∧				O		3
•	•	•	•	•	•	•	•	•		
O				∧				O		1

10 9 8 7 6 5 4 3 2 1

	k on RS, p on WS
•	P on RS, k on WS
O	Yarn over
∧	CDD (centered double decrease)

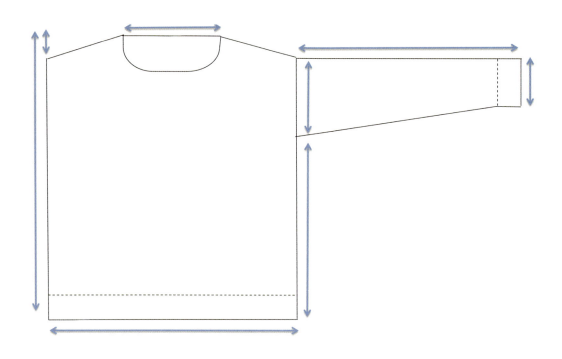

SCHEMATIC MEASUREMENTS

Back length 22 (22.75, 23.5, 23.75, 24.25)(24.75, 25.25, 25.75, 26.25)
Side seam (hem to underarm) 14"
Armhole depth 7 (7.5, 8, 8, 8.5)(9, 9.5, 9.5, 10)"
Shoulder drop 1 (1.25, 1.5, 1.75, 2)(2.25, 2.5, 2.75, 3)"
Finished bust circumference 37 (41, 46, 50, 54)(59, 63, 68, 72)"
Hem width (for blocking) 34.5 (38.75, 43, 47.25, 51.22)(55.5, 59.75, 64, 68.25)"
Shoulder width 5 (6, 7, 8, 9)(10, 11, 12, 13)"
Back neck width 7.75"
Sleeve length 16"
Upper arm diameter 13.5 (14.25, 15.5, 15.5, 16)(16.75, 17.75, 17.75, 18.5)
Cuff diameter 10.5 (11.25, 11.75, 11.75, 12.25)(11.75, 12.75, 12.75, 13.5)"

Green Mountain Spinnery

Green Mountain Spinnery began in a jail cell over 40 years ago, where two of its founders, who had been arrested for demonstrating against a nuclear power plant proposed for construction in New Hampshire, began to discuss how they could put their efforts into something positive for their community. For years, this core group worked together with a focus on thinking globally and acting locally, and out of that impetus arose the concept of a mill that would use locally grown wool. The learning curve was long and steep, but by December 1981, the Spinnery began to create yarn.

In many ways, not much has changed at the Spinnery over the past four decades. It has remained a worker-owned cooperative, and is still housed in its original location – a series of buildings cobbled together from what was originally a gas station. Inside, every nook and cranny of the rooms are filled with an assortment of machinery, ranging from antique to the latest technology, that scours, picks, cards, spins, steams, and plies the fiber as it journeys from raw wool to finished skeins of yarn. There is no automation here; each stage of the process requires a combination of mechanical and manual operation, and it's clear that learning how to operate, troubleshoot, and repair this bewildering array of equipment must have initially required a lot of trial and error.

The Spinnery has also remained true to its original guiding concepts of local, sustainable production. The mill is certified organic and it uses only natural fibers grown in North America, with a focus on locally grown New England wool and alpaca. About 30% of the yarn is milled for independent yarn makers and dyers, and the minimum is only 35 raw pounds of fiber, making it accessible for even small-batch producers. All of the yarns produced at the mill are woolen spun, in weights from lace to bulky, and in blends that include alpaca, mohair, and Tencel.

In the beginning, the Spinnery produced the majority of its yarn for outside customers, but now around 70% is milled for its own in-house label. The wool for all of its yarns except Cotton Comfort arrives bale-dyed, and the Spinnery blends its own colors in the milling process. There are over a dozen GMS yarns that range from Simply Fine, a single ply fingering weight wool and mohair blend, to Cotton Comfort, a DK weight blend of Targhee wool and organic cotton. Each of the yarns identifies not only the fiber content, but the specific sheep breeds; for instance, Weekend Wool "features a blend of the soft wools from Rambouillet, Columbia, Targhee and Friesian sheep mixed with the lustrous fleeces from Corriedale, Montadale and Romneys."

This is the type of information that customers have begun to ask for, notes Larisa Demos, one of the six employee-owners at the Spinnery. "People want to know what fibers are in the yarn. What breeds are used. Where it comes from, and whether it's local. I think it's a part of the larger farm-to-table movement, and the result has been a huge increase in people caring about where their yarn comes from." David Ritchie, one of original founders of the Spinnery, echoes this observation: "I feel that people have really become so sophisticated and educated about the variety of fibers. It used to be that knitters just hoped it was wool. Now, they're looking for wool from specific breeds of sheep that is domestically raised, dyed, and milled."

Green Mountain Spinnery

Website: spinnery.com

Address: 7 Brickyard Lane, Putney, VT

Phone: 1.800.321.9665

The departure station for the Conway Scenic Railroad (upper left), one of New Hampshire's 66 covered bridges (above right), autumn leaves on the Connecticut River (below left), and a cozy spot to read at Putney's Antidote Books (below right).

Shetland sheep graze near Green Mountain Spinnery (above left), ivy and brick is a common sight in Burlington, Vermont, along the shores of Lake Champlain (above right), and New Hampshire's Franconia Notch (bottom).

Falling Leaves
quilted leaf panels by Andrea Hungerford

I love using leaves or other botanicals in my making because it is like pressing a particular memory of a time and place into the fabric, along with the leaves. When I bring out the piece every autumn, I recall the particular season or location when it was made: who I was with and what I was doing. It's as if individual memories were impressed in the fabric, along with the leaf impressions. I bring these pieces out each year as the weather turns cooler to celebrate the coming of autumn and the changing of the seasons.

MATERIALS:
Paints: Liquitext Acrylic Color Basics in colors Red Oxide, Alizarin Crimson Hue, Primary Yellow, and Yellow Oxide

Fabric: Kona Cotton in color Bone (1.5 yards for front panels, 2.5 yards for back panels and binding)

Gutermann thread in Color #22 (or color to match fabric), and Colors #1800, 1661, and 4820 (or contrast colors that correspond with paint colors) (optional)

Low-loft batting (twin size or 50'' x 70'')

EQUIPMENT:
Rotary board and cutter
Scissors
Hand sewing needle
Paintbrush
Safety pins
Cardboard
Breyer (optional)
Free motion quilting sewing machine foot (optional)

NOTES:
Wash fabric first if you want to be able to wash your pieces once they're done (for instance, if you're going to use these techniques to create a quilt).

Pick your leaves immediately before you're ready to paint; fresh leaves will lie flat more easily and create a crisper impression in the paint.

If you are going to want to wash the finished piece (for instance, if you'd like to use this technique to make a quilt), you can add Martha Stewart Tintable Fabric Medium Paint to the acrylic paints. Combine one part fabric medium to two parts acrylic paint and follow the instructions on the fabric medium package to make sure that the paint won't fade or dissolve when washed.

CUTTING:
Four pieces (one for each panel), each 13.5" × 44".
Four pieces (one for each panel backing), each 17.5" × 48" (or approximately 2" larger than the panels on all four sides).
2" strips of binding: 8 strips 46" long and 8 strips 15.5" long.

PAINTING:
1. Put plastic or cardboard under the fabric panel so that the paint doesn't soak through to the table. Work with one panel at a time, laying it flat over the plastic or cardboard.

2. Lay the leaf flat on a separate piece of cardboard (or washable work space). Using a paintbrush, paint the back side of the leaf (the leaf veins are more visible and you'll get a better impression). Don't paint the leaf too heavily, or the details won't show up well in the impression.

3. Once the leaf is painted, lay it carefully on the fabric, put a clean sheet of paper over the leaf, and gently roll over it with a breyer (or press evenly with your hand).

4. You can use the same leaf two or even three times – each time you press, you'll get a more faded impression, which will give the appearance of depth and variety to your panel.

5. You can mix paint colors or dilute a color with white paint in order to create different color tones.

6. Once you've completed your leaf pressings on a panel, hang it to dry.

QUILTING:

1. For each panel, lay a backing piece down wrong side up, then layer on the batting, and then lay on the panel, right side up. You will have created a "sandwich", with the batting in the middle. Smooth the fabric to make sure there aren't any wrinkles on the top or bottom of the sandwich. (I like working with these smaller panels, as opposed to an entire quilt, if you're new to quilting, because it's easier to manipulate the pieces at this stage). Using safety pins, pin along all four sides and down the middle to secure the pieces together.

2. The panels are small enough that they don't have to be quilted – the batting won't shift around if you want to just go straight to binding. However, if you'd like to experiment with free motion quilting, and add to the design elements of the panels, use a contrasting thread color (or you can just use a color that matches the fabric, if you don't want the quilting to show much) and free motion quilt around the shape of some of the leaves (I chose six to eight leaves per panel). I used contrast color thread in my bobbin, as well, so that you can see the leaf shapes on the back side, but you could use thread that matches the fabric so that the quilting isn't as noticeable on the back side.

Free motion quilting tutorial: https://www.youtube.com/watch?v=ZCHLA1P43gw

3. After quilting, trim backing and batting so that edges are even with the panel. Use 2" strips to bind quilt.

Quilt binding tutorial: https://leahday.com/pages/how-to-bind-a-quilt-by-machine

4. Press binding for a smooth finish (be sure not to touch the hot iron to any of the painted sections of the panels).

5. Create a sleeve for each of the panels and hand-stitch on to the back (so stitches don't show through to the front), so that the panels can be hung on a rod.

Quilt sleeve tutorial: *https://www.quiltweek.com/hanging-sleeve-instructions/*

You can use these same techniques for a myriad of other fabric projects. For instance, use a single large piece of fabric (or stitch the panels together) to make a quilt. Finish your panels with backing (but no batting) and use as table runners. Or, don't use batting or backing and leave the panel edges raw for a completely different look as a wall hanging, table runner, or place mats.

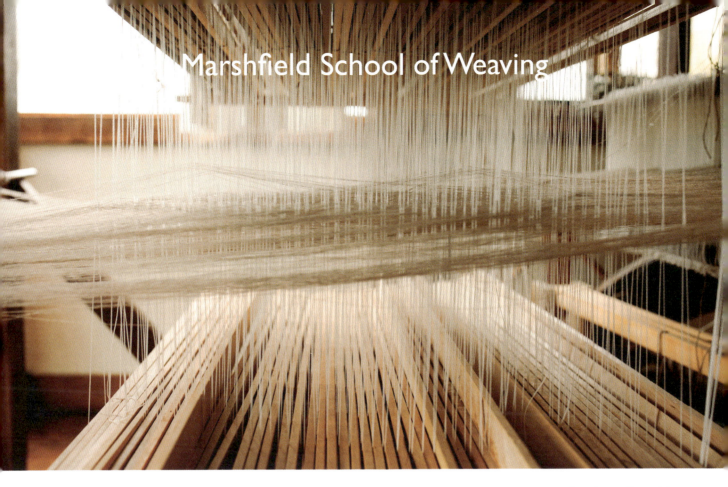

Marshfield School of Weaving

In the wooded hills of rural Vermont sits a 19th century barn that houses the largest collection of working 18th and 19th century looms in the country. It also houses Marshfield School of Weaving, which for over 40 years has taught textiles techniques practiced in 18th century Britain and early America to students who travel from all over the world.

Marshfield is unique in its traditional approach to handweaving on historic equipment. The School was founded in 1974 by Norman Kennedy, whose vision was to keep alive the traditions he learned from the last of the hand weavers in his native land of Scotland. Yet Marshfield is also unique in that it sits at the intersection between historical tradition and the modern-day need for connection, sustainability, and the creation of something of meaning and substance. "People have a need to create," reflects Marshfield Director Kate Smith. "What they learn here isn't only weaving. It's better for the planet, and it's better for the psyche and the soul. People need to be closer to the primary things of life like the clothes on their back."

Kate's vision for Marshfield is that it continue to preserve the traditional ways of the past, while at the same time, make those skills relevant for the future. To that end, she is moving in the direction of using only sustainable materials on the loom. "We're moving away from yarn that isn't sustainibly grown or processed. In Norman's day, you grew your flax, raised your sheep, and spun and wove what you'd grown and raised." Ultimately, Kate hopes to use primarily fibers that are locally produced.

Marshfield offers beginning to advanced weaving classes, as well as workshops on natural dyeing, spinning, printing and other textile techniques. The School periodically brings in guest instructors, and is looking to

expand its roster. Current classes vary in length, but when the school first opened, students came for intensive six-week classes. "You were given a fleece when you arrived," Kate recalls, "and you learned how to do everything — washing, carding, dyeing, spinning, and weaving. You were part of the entire process, from start to finish." Kate has also initiated a research center that has hosted a textile history forum and a spinning wheel symposium. "I want to gather all of these great people, with all of their knowledge, in one place, where they can share with each other."

By embracing its historical roots and its traditional approach to making cloth, Marshfield can be part of the larger movement toward slow, conscious fashion.

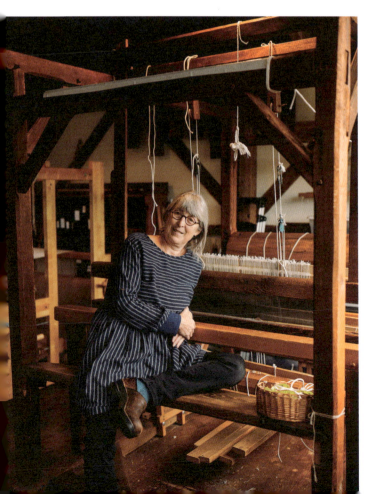

"It's about changing people's entire consciousness about consuming and possessions," Kate explains. "If we had only two pairs of jeans in our wardrobe, we could spend $500 to pay the cost of having those jeans sustainibly made. I'd like to challenge my students: in five years, we wear only the clothes we make. That's where I would like to see the future of the school – not just preserving these techniques and equipment, which is valuable in itself, but also to take a greater activist role in the world."

Marshfield School of Weaving

Website: marshfieldschoolofweaving.com

Address: 589 Eaton Cemetery Rd, Marshfield, VT

E-mail: info@MarshfieldSchoolofWeaving.com

Instagram: marshfieldschoolofweaving

Winter Light

by Nataliya Volyanyuk

SIZING
Women's S/M (L/XL)
Approx chest measurement 30–38 (40–44)"
Shown in Size M with approx ± 14" ease

FINISHED MEASUREMENTS
Chest Circumference: 48 (58)"
Back Length: 23.5 (24.5)"

MATERIALS
Harrisville Silk & Wool (30% Silk/70% Fine Wool, 175 yds per 50 g), 9 (10) skeins in Veronica
US 6 (4 mm) 40" circular needles and DPNs, waste yarn or stitch holder, tapestry needle

GAUGE
19 sts and 28 rows = 4" in Stockinette Stitch, blocked

NOTES
Cardigan is knit flat from the top down, starting with a collar in Ribbing Pattern. Stitches are picked up along the edge of the collar to form the back, shoulders, and fronts. Fronts are worked in Ribbing Pattern, while back and sleeves are worked in Stockinette Stitch. Body ends in 2×2 ribbing. Sleeves end in 1×1 ribbing. Pockets are picked up from held stitches and worked after the body is complete. Sleeves are picked up and worked in the round, starting with short-row shaping for the cap.

RIBBING PATTERN
Row 1 (RS): *K2, p2; rep until one stitch left, k1.
Row 2 (WS): *P2, k2; rep until one stitch left, p1.

DIRECTIONS
Collar
Using your choice of provisional cast on, CO 53 sts.
Mark RS of the knitting with stitch marker, work Rows 1 & 2 of Ribbing Pattern 17 (20) times. Place sts on holder or scrap yarn. Do not cut yarn.

Unravel provisional cast on. Join new ball of yarn with RS facing and begin Ribbing Pattern on a RS row. Work Rows 1 & 2 of Ribbing Pattern 17 (20) times. Place sts on holder or scrap yarn. Cut yarn.

Upper Body
Place held sts with working yarn st attached on needle work 53 collar stitches in Ribbing Pattern, then evenly pick up 56 (64) stitches from the long edge of the collar, and then work other held Collar sts in Row 1 of Ribbing Pattern.

Set-Up Row (WS): Work Ribbing Pattern Row 2 for 53 stitches, pm (end of band ribbing), p1, pm (shoulder), p2 (shoulder seam), pm (start back), p50 (58), pm (end back), p2 (shoulder seam), pm, p1, pm (start band ribbing), work Ribbing Pattern Row 2 to end of row.

Row 1 (RS): Work Ribbing Pattern Row 1 to m, sm, k1, M1R, sm, k2, sm, M1L, knit to m, M1R, sm, k2, sm, M1L, k1, sm, work Ribbing Pattern to end of row. 166 (174) sts.

Row 2 (WS): Work Ribbing Pattern Row 2 to m, sm, p1, k1, MIR, sm, p2, sm, MIL, purl to m, MIR, sm, p2, sm, MIL, k2, sm, work Ribbing Pattern to end of row. 170 (178) sts.

Row 3: Work Ribbing Pattern Row 1 to m, sm, cont Ribbing Pattern as established to m, MIR, sm, k2, sm, MIL, knit to m, MIR, sm, k2, sm, MIL, cont Ribbing Pattern as established sm, work Ribbing Pattern to end of row. 4 sts inc'd.

Row 4: Work Ribbing Pattern Row 2 to m, sm, cont Ribbing Pattern as established to m, MIR, sm, p2, sm, MIL, purl to m, MIR, sm, p2, sm, MIL, cont Ribbing Pattern as established to m, sm, work Ribbing Pattern to end of row. 4 sts inc'd.

Rep last 2 rows 13 (17) more times. 282 (322) sts; 110 (134) sts for Back, 2 sts for each Shoulder, 31 (39) sts for each Front, 53 sts for each band.

Cont working increases to Fronts and Back every RS row as follows:

Row 1 (RS): Work Ribbing Pattern Row 1 to m, sm, cont Ribbing Pattern as established to m, MIR, sm, k2, sm, MIL, knit to m, MIR, sm, k2, sm, MIL, cont Ribbing Pattern as established sm, work Ribbing Pattern to end of row. 4 sts inc'd.

Row 2 (WS): Work Ribbing Pattern Row 2 to m, sm, cont Ribbing Pattern to m, sm, p2, sm, purl to m, sm, p2, work Ribbing Pattern to m, sm, work Ribbing Pattern to end of row.

Rep last 2 rows once more. 290 (330) sts; 114 (138) sts for Back, 2 sts for each Shoulder, 33 (41) sts for each Front, 53 sts for each band.

Divide Fronts and Back as follows:

Next Row (RS): Work Ribbing Pattern Row 1 to the marker, sm, cont Ribbing Pattern as established to 1 st before m, MIR, k1, place shoulder stitches, back stitches and right front stitches on scrap yarn and continue working only on left front. 87 (95) sts for Left Front and band.

Left Front
Row 1 (WS): P1, work Ribbing Pattern Row 2 to marker, sm, cont

Ribbing Pattern as established to end of row.

Row 2 (RS): Work Ribbing Pattern Row 1 to the marker, sm, cont Ribbing Pattern as established to 1 st before end of Row, M1R, k1. 1 st inc'd.

Rep last 2 rows 3 more times, then work Row 1 once more. 91 (99) sts for Front and Band.

Cont working increases ever other RS row as follows:

Row 1 (RS): Work Ribbing Pattern Row 1 to the marker, sm, cont Ribbing Pattern as established to 1 st before end of row, k1.

Row 2 (WS): P1, work Ribbing Pattern Row 2 to marker, sm, cont Ribbing Pattern as established to end of row.

Row 3 (RS): Work Ribbing Pattern Row 1 to the marker, sm, cont Ribbing Pattern as established to 1 st before end of Row, M1R, k1. 1 st inc'd.

Row 4: Rep Row 2.

Rep last 4 rows 2 more times. Final 2 sts on the RS row should be k2. 94 (102) sts for Front and Band.

Cont working in Ribbing pattern for 12 (22) rows. Place all left front stitches on scrap yarn and leave the ball attached.

Right Front

Return held Right Front sts to needles and join yarn with RS facing. 86 (94) sts for Front and Band.

Row 1 (RS): K1, M1L, work Ribbing Pattern Row 1 to marker, sm, cont Ribbing Pattern to end of row. 1 st inc'd.

Row 2 (WS): Work Ribbing Pattern Row 2 to marker, sm, cont Ribbing Pattern to last st, p1.

Rep last 2 rows 4 more times. 91 (99) sts for Front and Band.

Cont working increases ever other RS row as follows:

Row 1 (RS): K1, work Ribbing Pattern Row 1 to marker, sm, cont Ribbing Pattern to end of row.

Row 2 (WS): Work Ribbing Pattern Row 2 to marker, sm, cont Ribbing Pattern to last st, p1.

Row 3 (RS): K1, M1L, work Ribbing Pattern Row 1 to marker, sm, cont Ribbing Pattern to end of row. 1 st inc'd.

Row 4 (WS): Rep Row 2.

Rep last 4 rows 2 more times. First 2 sts on the RS row should be k2. 94 (102) sts for Front and Band.

Cont working in Ribbing pattern for 12 (22) rows. Place all left front stitches on scrap yarn and leave the ball attached.

Upper Back

Leave shoulders stitches on scrap yarn and return 114 (138) Back sts to needle, joining yarn with RS facing. Work in St st for 34 (44) rows, cut yarn.

Body

Join Fronts and Back for Body as follows:

Row 1 (RS): Return Left Front Sts to working needle and, using attached yarn, work Ribbing Pattern to marker, sm, cont Ribbing Pattern as established until 1 st left on Left Front, pm, k1, CO 4 sts, k all back stitches, CO 4 sts, k1 from Right Front, pm, work Ribbing Pattern to marker, sm, cont Ribbing Pattern as established to end of row.

Row 2 (WS): Work Ribbing Pattern to m, sm, cont in Ribbing pattern as established to m, sm, purl to m, sm, cont in Ribbing Pattern to m, sm, cont in Ribbing pattern to end of row.

Work even in Ribbing Pattern and St st until Back measures 9" from underarm CO sts.

Pocket Slots
Row 1 (RS): Working Ribbing Pattern to m, sm, work in Ribbing Pattern for 3 (7) sts, place next 32 sts on scrap yarn, CO 32 sts, cont in Ribbing Pattern as established to m, sm, knit to m, sm, work in Ribbing Pattern for 5 (9) sts, place next 32 sts on scrap yarn, CO 32 sts, cont in Ribbing Pattern as established to m, sm, cont in Ribbing pattern to end of row.
Row 2 (WS): Work Ribbing Pattern to m, sm, cont in Ribbing pattern as established to m, sm, purl to m, sm, cont in Ribbing Pattern to m, sm, cont in Ribbing pattern to end of row.

Continue working as established previously – fronts panel in ribbing pattern to the markers and back in stockinette for 5" (13 cm) ending with wrong side row.

Bottom Ribbing
Row 1 (RS): Work Ribbing Pattern to m, sm, cont in Ribbing pattern as established to m, sm, k1, (p2, k2) to 3 sts before m, p2, k1, sm, cont in Ribbing Pattern to m, sm, cont in Ribbing pattern to end of row.
Row 2 (WS): Work Ribbing Pattern to m, sm, cont in Ribbing pattern as established to m, sm, p1, (k2, p2) to 3 sts before m, k2, p1, sm, cont in Ribbing Pattern to m, sm, cont in Ribbing pattern to end of row.

Rep last 2 rows for 1.5". BO all sts in pattern.

Pocket linings

Pick up 32 stitches reserved for pockets from scrap yarn. Knit 5'' (13 cm) in ribbing pattern as established previously, BO.

Sew pocket linings to back of cardigan.

Sleeves

Rnd 1: Beginning at center of underarm CO, PU and k3 stitches then from underarm CO (one in each CO st and one to close the gap with the Body), PU and k25 (33) sts along sleeve opening, k2 held shoulder stitches, then PU and k25 (33) sts along sleeve opening, then PU and k3 sts from underarm CO. PM and join to work in the round. 58 (74) sts.

Shape Sleeve Cap

Row 1 (RS): K39 (51), work GSR.
Row 2 (WS): P19 (27), work GSR.
Row 3: Knit to 2 (3) sts past previous GSR, knitting GSR ds tog, work GSR.
Row 4: Purl to 2 (3) sts past previous GSR, purling GSR ds tog, work GSR.
Rep last 2 rows 6 (5) more times. Knit to end of rnd.
Knit 6 rnds.
Decrease round: K, k2tog, knit to 4 sts before m, ssk, k2. 2 sts dec'd; 56 (72) sts.
Rep Dec Rnd every 10 rnds 6 more times. 44 (60) sts.
Cont in St st until Sleeve measures 10'' (25 cm) from underarm CO. Work (k1,p1) ribbing for 26 rounds. BO all stitches.

FINISHING

Weave in ends and block to measurements.

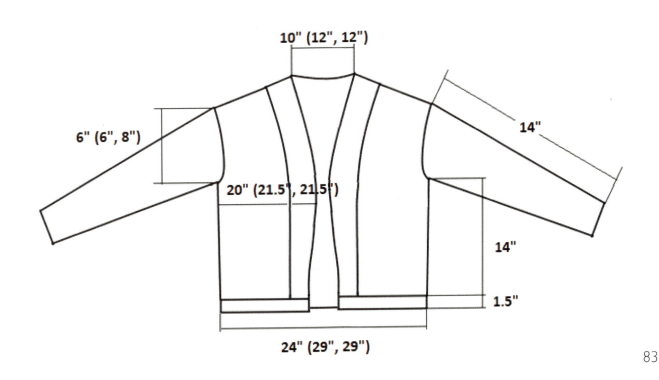

Beside the Betsie (fabric collage)
Photograph by Lori Landau

Dianne Shullenberger

No matter the time of year, Dianne Shullenberger can be found exploring the outdoors. Every day, regardless of weather or season, she walks through the forests, rides her bike, or, skis through freshly fallen snow, finding daily meditation in the Vermont countryside. All of this can be found right out her front door, and it's this easy access to nature that inspires Dianne's art. She loves each of the seasons, and particularly the transitions between seasons — brief moments of almost continuous change, when the smallest details become visible. How leaves curl after the first frost, the touch of color in flower buds in early spring, even how the quality of light changes day to day. Because Dianne is outside every day, she notices these subtle changes in her surroundings and reflects them in her work.

Like the minute changes in her natural environment, Dianne's art is comprised of many small, subtle details. Her works are composed of bits and pieces — individual pencil strokes, minuscule pieces of fabric — and it takes time and attention to appreciate the effort and focus that have gone into creating them. The combination of all of these tiny components creates an image greater than the sum of its parts, with a texture and complexity that mimics the real world in an intimate way.

Dianne is a warm and welcoming host as she tours us around her studio and explains how her art is created. We get to peek into her impressively large fabric stash, overflowing drawers of thread, and small momentoes that she has collected over the years. Dianne has an easy, natural way of connecting with people, and it's evident that she is a gifted instructor, as well as an accomplished artist.

The first step in Dianne's process is to take photographs, so that she captures a moment in time before it changes. In the summer, these photos are often the basis for her work with colored pencils. But in the winter, when she has more time to spend indoors, she turns to fiber and fabric. Originally a quilter, "I wanted something more organic and wild," she recalls. "I started ripping fabric, balling it up, plastering it down, going over it with thread." The base of her pieces is acid-free tissue paper, because "it's the thinnest way to start. If I start with fabric, it gets too thick. Once it's all stitched, I just peel the paper away and it leaves these natural, organic raw edges."

Dianne first builds the bigger blocks of color, then hones in with smaller and smaller pieces of fabric. She doesn't cut out specific shapes, but instead forms images by combining many small pieces of fabric. The variety of fabric colors and textures is dizzying, and each serves a purpose; for instance, sheer fabrics can overlay others to create a foggy, misty atmosphere. Then, once multiple layers of fabric are in place, "thread becomes a much bigger player," she explains. "The very last step is what I call drawing with thread." Many of Dianne's fabric pieces comprise a series of works, such as After the Frost, Listening to Rocks, and Pond Patterns. Recently, she's been photographing "quiet water" and has plans for a new series that examines different marshes, bogs, and fens.

Dianne's studio was built as an addition to the historical home where she and her family have lived for close to 40 years, and it houses a first floor gallery, with a light-filled studio above. Three large windows overlook the pond where her children (and now grandchildren) swim in the summer and ice skate in the winter. "This

Dianne Shullenberger

Website: dianneshullenberger.com

E-mail: VtDianne@hotmail.com

is a peaceful, calm place to work, with everything at my fingertips that I want to see and do," she reflects. "I'm always being exposed to new subject matters just outside these windows, and I never run out of inspiration. Usually there are so many ideas in my head that I can't get them all out fast enough!"

Golden Afternoon Mittens

by Angela Tong

These beautiful cabled mittens will make winter much more bearable. The mittens will keep you warm and add a colorful accessory to your wardrobe. There are so many wonderful colors of Harrisville Highland yarn to choose from! This wool wears exceptionally well and should last you many years.

FINISHED MEASUREMENTS
Finished 6.5 (8, 9)" hand circumference, 6.5 (8.25, 9.5)" tall
Model is wearing 8" size

MATERIALS
Harrisville Highland (100% wool; 200 yds per 100 g): #04 Gold, 1 skein
US 5 (3.75 mm) and US 7 (4.5 mm) DPNs (adjust needle size if necessary to obtain correct gauge)
Tapestry needle, markers, cable needle, waste yarn for thumb

GAUGE
20 sts and 30 rnds = 4" in Stockinette Stitch, blocked

NOTES
The mitts are worked in the round from the bottom up, starting at the cuff. The thumb is finished last.

DIRECTIONS: RIGHT MITTEN
Cuff
With smaller needles, CO 32 (40, 44) sts and divide onto 4 dpns. Place marker (pm) for beg of rnd and join for working in the rnd, being careful not to twist sts.

Ribbing Rnd: *K1, p1; rep from * to end. Rep the last rnd until the cuff measures 1.75 (2, 2.25)".

Change to larger needles
Inc Rnd: K to last st, M1L, k1. 1 st inc'd, 33 (41, 45) sts.

Shape Thumb Gusset
Set-up Rnd: K16 (20, 22) sts, pm, M1L, k1, M1R, pm, k to end. 2 sts inc'd.
Rnd 1: Knit.
Rnd 2: K2 (4, 5), C4B, k4, C4F, k to end.
Rnd 3: K to m, sm, M1L, k to next m, M1R, sm, k to end. 2 sts inc'd.
Rnds 4 & 5: Knit.
Rnd 6: K4 (6, 7), C4F, C4B, k to m, M1L, sm, k to next m, M1R, k to end. 2 sts inc'd.
Rnds 7 & 8: Knit.
Last 8 rnds 2 (2, 3) times total.
Total gusset sts between markers 11 (11, 15) sts.

Hand
Set-Up: K to m, place gusset sts onto scrap yarn, remove markers, CO 1 using Backward Loop Cast On, k to end 33 (41, 45) sts. Pm for beg of rnd.

Rnd 1: K2 (4, 5), C4B, k4, C4F, k to end.
Rnds 2–4: Knit.

Rnd 5: K4 (6, 7), C4F, C4B, k to end
Rnds 6–8: Knit.
Works Rnds 1–8 until hand measures 4 (5.5, 6.5)" from the top of the ribbing.

Shape Top
Rnd 1: K16 (20, 22), pm, k2tog, k to end. 1 st dec'd, 32 (40, 44) sts.
Rnd 2: (Ssk, k to 3 sts before m, k2tog, k1) twice. 4 sts dec'd.
Work Rnd 2 a total of 5 (7, 8) times. 12 (12, 12) sts.

Break yarn, leaving a 6" tail to thread through remaining live sts. Pull tight to close top of mitten. Weave in ends on the inside.

Thumb
Place gussets sts onto larger needles. Pick up and knit 1 st at gap, knit to end, pm to mark beg of rnd 12 (12, 16) sts.
Join and work in St st until thumb measures 1 (1.5, 1.75)" from pickup rnd.

Shape Top of Thumb
Rnd 1: [K2tog, k2 (2, 3)] 2 times, k2tog, k2 (2, 4). 3 sts dec'd, 9 (9, 13) sts.
Rnds 2 & 3: Knit.
Rnd 4: K1, *k2tog; rep from * to end. 5 (5, 7) sts.

Break yarn, leaving a 6" tail to thread through remaining live sts. Pull tight to close top of mitten. Weave in ends on the inside.

DIRECTIONS: LEFT MITTEN
Work as for Right Mitten Cuff.

Change to larger needles
K to last st, M1L, k1. 1 st inc'd, 33 (41, 45) sts.

Shape Thumb Gusset
Set-up Rnd: K16 (20, 22) sts, pm, M1L, k1, M1R, pm, k to end. 2 sts inc'd.
Rnd 1: Knit.
Rnd 2: K to m, sm, k to m, sm, k2 (4, 5), C4B, k4, C4F, k to end.
Rnd 3: K to m, sm, M1L, k to next m, M1R, sm, k to end. 2 sts inc'd.
Rnds 4 & 5: Knit.
Rnd 6: K to m, sm, M1L, k to m, M1R, sm, k4 (6, 7), C4F, C4B, k to end. 2 sts inc'd.
Rnds 7 & 8: Knit.
Rep last 8 rnds 2 (2, 3) times total.
Total gusset sts between markers 11 (11, 15) sts.

Hand
Set-Up: K to m, place gusset sts onto scrap yarn, remove markers, CO 1 Using Backward Loop Cast On, k to end 33 (41, 45) sts. Pm for beg of rnd.

Rnd 1: K19 (25, 28), C4B, k4, C4F, k to end.
Rnds 2–4: Knit.
Rnd 5: K21 (27, 30), C4F, C4B, k to end
Rnd 6–8: Knit.
Works Rnds 1–8 until hand measures 4 (5.5, 6.5)'' from the top of the ribbing.

Work Shape Top, Thumb, Shape Top of Thumb as for Right Mitten.

FINISHING
Weave in all ends and block lightly.

Glossary

ABBREVIATIONS

1/1 LC	slip 1 stitch on cable needle hold in front, knit 1, knit 1 from cable needle
1/1 LPC	slip 1 stitch on cable needle hold in front, purl 1, knit 1 from cable needle
1/1 RC	slip 1 stitch on cable needle hold in back, knit 1, knit 1 from cable needle
1/1 RPC	slip 1 stitch on cable needle hold in back, knit 1, purl 1 from cable needle
BO	bind off
CC	contrast color
CO	cast on
dec(s/'d)	decrease(s)/decreased
ds	double stitches
GSR	German short rows (see Techniques)
inc(s/'d)	increase(s)/increased
k	knit
k2tog	knit 2 together
m	marker
m1	make 1: with right needle, pick up running thread between needles from back to front and place it on left needle, then knit it through the back loop
m1P	make 1 purl: with right needle, pick up running thread between needles from front to back, place on left needle, purl it through the front loop.
MC	main color
p	purl
p2tog	purl 2 together
patt	pattern
pm	place marker
rem	remain(s)
rep	repeat
RS	right side
Sl1	slip 1 stitch purlwise with yarn in front
sm	slip market
ssk	[slip 1 as if to knit] 2 times, insert left needle into fronts of these sts and knit them together
St st	stockinette stitch
st(s)	stitch(es)
WS	wrong side

TECHNIQUES

German Short-Rows tutorial: https://www.purlsoho.com/create/german-short-rows/

Three-Needle Bind-Off: https://www.purlsoho.com/create/3-needle-bind-off/

Buttonholes: https://www.masondixonknitting.com/techniques-depth-making-buttonholes/

A perfect fall day along the shores of Lake Winnipesaukee, New Hampshire's largest lake.